"I would have KILLED — literally killed — to have had this book as a teenager! Build me a time machine, and I will fly back to high school right now to give myself this book with a note saying, 'See — you CAN do this... and you can start today.' For any budding Steven Spielberg or J. J. Abrams — or their parents — this book should be the start of a long, exciting career."

> — Chad Gervich, author, *Small Screen, Big Picture: A Writer's Guide to the TV Business* and TV writer/producer (*Wipeout, Foody Call, Reality Binge, Speeders*)

"This is the book teenagers will enjoy as well as take information to make those camcorder films more than loving hands at home. I recommended the book on my show and everyone of the crew members wanted one. Even if it says for 'Teenagers' it could also be for any age."

> — Connie Martinson, host of Talk Books

"*Filmmaking for Teens, 2nd Ed.* makes for an easy read with loads of information in a concise way. This book will give you the edge you need to get a jump-start into the world of film. A perfect book for starting filmmakers."

> — Erin Corrado, *www.onemoviefiveviews.com*

"We had the pleasure of having Troy Lanier teach at the Academy the last few summers and what a treat it was! One of Troy's many talents lies in his ability to communicate with 'kids.' Whether it's to inspire or educate, his voice resonates with young filmmakers. In *Pulling Off Your Shorts* that same spirit is captured, along with clear and concise methods that will empower young filmmakers everywhere to respond to the challenge of following their dreams and becoming the best filmmaker they can be!"

> — Christopher Watkins, director, New England Film Academy

"*Filmmaking for Teens* is an exceptional filmmaking guide for anyone determined to create their own film. Written by Troy Lanier and Clay Nichols, *Filmmaking for Teens* is a simple, easy to understand guide to improving amateur videos. With tips from how to create a five-minute film to an introduction of a broad range of film equipment, this book is not only well organized, but also cunning, comical, and engaging. It's the perfect book to have handy during any production!"

> — Amanda Porter, associate editor, *School Video News*

"For any students wishing to learn about film or already studying the art, this book is a great resource. I especially appreciated the section on asking for money — last year the director of the film I worked on made his crew pay for everything."

> — Madison Ball, Junior, Class of 2011, St. Stephen's Episcopal School, Austin, Texas

"This book is fast and furious, and funny. It is jammed with great craft ideas spanning the spectrum of filmmaking. The authors obviously have a ton of experience, because they offer wonderfully practical considerations like the '5-Minute Rule' and their suggestion that writers 'Don't Interrogate the Draft'."

> — Mike Dolan, director, film teacher, St. Stephen's Episcopal School, Austin, Texas.

"Redesigned to be even easier to understand and packed with more up-to-date information on digital filmmaking, the 2nd edition of *Filmmaking for Teens* should be the essential textbook for schools and community centers that want to provide a high-quality filmmaking curriculum for their students."

> — Jeremy Hanke, editor-in-chief, *MicroFilmmaker* Magazine

"Steven Spielberg started his directing career when he was 12, shooting Westerns on 8mm film. Now any aspiring young filmmaker can use a consumer video camera, Final Cut and YouTube to break in too. *Filmmaking for Teens* is a 7-11 full of every filmmaking goodie you'll need to write, shoot, edit, and show a short film that people will actually want to see, using the resources you already have: friends, parents, no money, and a long weekend. From how to finish a script, to when to go handheld, to how to mooch equipment, to what won't work, this book is all you need to get your filmmaking career started."

> — Alex Epstein, author, *Crafty Screenwriting* and *Crafty TV Writing*, co-writer of the hit comedy film *Bon Cop Bad Cop*

"*Filmmaking for Teens* provides sensible, doable guidelines to make possible a movie project. This encouraging book is a quick, fun read as it gives planning tips, exercises, and lots of photos of teens at work. Study this book, grab a camera, and rock 'n' roll — er, maybe hip-hop."

> — Mary J. Schirmer, screenwriter and instructor

filmmaking
for teens
PULLING OFF YOUR SHORTS

TROY LANIER &
CLAY NICHOLS

Published by Michael Wiese Productions
12400 Ventura Blvd, Suite 1111
Studio City, CA 91604
tel. 818.379.8799
fax 818.986.3408
mw@mwp.com
www.mwp.com

Cover Design: MWP
Interior Book Design: Gina Mansfield Design
Editor: Paul Norlen

Printed by McNaughton & Gunn, Inc., Saline, Michigan
Manufactured in the United States of America

Library of Congress Cataloging-in-Publication Data

Lanier, Troy, 1967-
 Filmmaking for teens : pulling off your shorts / Troy Lanier & Clay Nichols.
    p. cm.
 Includes index.
 ISBN 978-1-932907-68-1
 1. Short films--Production and direction. I. Nichols, Clay, 1967- II. Title.
 PN1995.9.P7L29 2010
 791.4302'3--dc22
                                    2009029891

TABLE OF
CONTENTS

ACKNOWLEDGMENTS

The authors would like to thank Ken Lee and Michael Wiese for their continued support of this project, Paul Norlen for patiently shepherding it to a second conclusion, and Gina Mansfield for making it look so good. Thanks to the DadLabs cast and crew for giving us the time and space to include what we learned there in this book. And a special thanks to Erica De Leon for her help in the preparation of this manuscript.

(FAST)
FOREWORD

Casting Call!

Is this book for you?

Are you...

A teenager who:

▶ loves movies
▶ has dreamed about making movies yourself
▶ is observant or hilarious or insightful or a little weird or all of the above
▶ is interested in an experience that is exciting, creative, and the hardest fun you've ever had
▶ wants to impress and entertain friends, family, college admissions officers, film festival judges, movie industry moguls, and audiences worldwide

or an adult who:
▶ is a parent, grandparent, or friend of a teenager
▶ is interested in supporting a young person's creativity and encouraging a positive, teambuilding, educational activity
▶ is a teacher hoping to guide students step-by-step through the filmmaking process

Answer yes to any of these? Then head for the register, dude.

Because this book can help teens to realize their filmmaking dreams, transforming them into that mythical film-world figure, the slash — a writer/producer/director/editor.

This funny and irreverent how-to takes young would-be filmmakers from the moment of inspiration to a finished short film and beyond. Young auteurs-in-training learn everything they need to do, step-by-step, to craft their first movie.

With tips and techniques on brainstorming, screenwriting, scheduling, shooting, editing, and marketing, this accessible, hip, and complete guide will nurture and inspire a new generation of filmmakers.

Using our prescription, you can pull off your shorts in just a few months with a reasonable commitment of time, widely available technology, and just a few dollars.

See you at Sundance.

Rolling... and... action!

INTRODUCTION

ROLL CREDITS

Welcome to the beginning of your filmmaking career.

It's an exciting moment, isn't it, imagining what lies ahead. The fame. The stretch Hummer. Chatting at the premiere with Ashton and Demi.

Okay, now wake up.

Because right now, at this moment, millions of teenagers all over the world are having the same fantasy. For most, that's where the story ends. It's just something to think about during English class when the teacher is droning on about Hawthorne (Demi starred in a movie based on that guy's book by the way). Making movies is something that almost everyone says they're interested in. They're thinking about. They actually have a really cool idea.

Almost everyone has dreamed about strolling down the red carpet at one time or another, why else would people buy People. How many slobs sprawl on their sofas watching E! thinking that should be me? How many people have scrutinized movies or TV thinking, I could do that better? How may thousands of people are out there fantasizing about making movies as you read this book? And they're a little pathetic, aren't they. Because all they will ever do is dream.

But you are going to be different. Why? Because you are going to stop dreaming and start creating. You are going to be a filmmaker. What distinguishes a filmmaker from a dreamer is the plain fact that a filmmaker actually makes films. Finish a film, and you become one of a select few.

We've got some ideas on the subject of joining the select company of filmmakers. Our opinions come from making lots of films with young filmmakers. In the process, we've made or observed more mistakes than you can imagine. Our hope is that our screw-ups will be your gain. Anything we warn you against is probably something we've done. That's actually a good thing for you.

So we're opinionated. We think you'll be best off if you follow all the ideas we lay out in this book. We also realize that rules are meant to be broken. Because of practicalities, or unforeseen obstacles, or maybe because you're just plain difficult (lots of filmmakers are), you may not want to follow all the rules laid out in this book. More power to you.

For us, there is only one central and unavoidable rule:

Finish the film.

That's it. Our main idea. Nothing is more important than actually getting a movie done. Grand concepts, gorgeous ideas, and bust-a-gut premises by themselves are worth zippo. Your ideas only become something if they are realized. Or, in moviemaking lingo, it's nothing until it's "in the can." Above all else, you need to get it done. If only it were as simple as it sounds.

This book will guide you to becoming a filmmaker, or rather a writer/producer/director/editor by walking you through the production process from concept to distribution of your short film. We will take you from the desire to be a filmmaker to actually being one. From scratch to screen.

We will show you nothing less than how to pull off your shorts.

CHAPTER **1**

THE
KEYCHAIN

In our opinion there are six keys to getting your film finished:

1) Make a five-minute film.
2) Have a completed script before shooting.
3) Be a slash (writer/director/producer/editor).
4) Geek Out.
5) Use the three-day shooting schedule.
6) Edit on a deadline.

KEY 1 — FIVE-MINUTE RULE

It is our belief that you raise the odds of finishing your movie, of pulling off your shorts, if you tackle a project of reasonable size. Therefore, it is the premise of this guidebook that you should begin your career with a "short." We suggest a five-minute film.

"Five minutes?" you ask, perhaps out loud, attracting stares from other Starbucks patrons. You start to think about things that take five minutes: making a bowl of ramen, brushing your teeth, going to your locker for your books — none of which sound very much like your Hollywood dreams.

Five minutes? I can't go to the bathroom in five minutes.

What can I possibly do in five minutes?

A good little bit.

In five minutes you can tell a story that makes people laugh or cry or both. In five minutes you can show people something unique, take them someplace they have never been before. In five minutes you can communicate a lot about what you think and who you are. And for five minutes you can keep the attention of a jittery YouTube viewer.

You can say a lot in five minutes, and you can get it finished.

KEY 2 — SCRIPTED IN ADVANCE

Most kids, mostly those that never get past the dreaming phase, feel like film-making starts when they push the red button on their new camcorder. And to tell the truth, making it up as you go along can yield some hilarious results. You may have already made some improvisational films before ever reading this book, and you probably taught yourself some useful lessons, gained some great experience in the process.

The problem with improvised films is that they usually have that homemade, America's Funniest Animals look. And the humor is often of the "you-had-to-be-there" variety. It's always funnier if you know the people. To find a wider audience, to get your film and yourself noticed, to make it to the next level, you need profes-sional polish. To achieve a professional polish, you need good preparation and focus on the set. In order to prepare and focus, you need a script.

Having a script allows you to create a "set" in advance — a place where you can control things like lighting and sound. Creating the script forces you to sharpen and distill your story, so your audience will hear clearly what you have to say.

The script is also a tangible sign of how serious you are about making this film. You can use the script to recruit friends, teachers and parents, all the people you will need to make your movie. Ask a friend to be in your movie and he'll say, "Yeah, sure dude." Give him a script, and he'll actually show up.

KEY 3 — SLASH AND BURN

We assume that you will be the driving force behind the movies you will create. In the process of being "the woman" (or "man") and making this movie, you will have to wear so many hats your hair will start to fall out (this might also result from the stress of filmmaking). The most significant roles you will play will be those of writer, producer, director, and editor (you'll also be marketing director, location scout, and caterer). On this project you will be what is known affection-ately (or not) as a "Slash" aka a writer/producer/director/editor.

As a slash-writer, we will help you find a concept that fits the size of your project, and we will also give you exercises to refine your idea and get it down on paper. We'll give you the proper format and guide you toward a script that tells your story effectively.

As slash-producer, we will help you to think through and work out the galaxy of details that go into making even a short film. It is the producer's job to make sure that the director has everything she needs when the actual shooting starts, and to handle any unforeseen problems that may come up on the spot. The producer wrangles the equipment, sets the schedule, sweet-talks the owner of the location, recruits and manages the crew, and a million other things.

As a slash-director, we'll give you some preparation to be the master and com-mander of the film set. The director is the creator but also the decision maker. She calls the shots, what kind of shot, how many shots of the same scene — who and what goes where. But she must also carefully manage actors and the many collaborators without whom it would be impossible to finish the film.

As a slash-editor we will help you master the technology that makes professional looking films. Movie types often say that "movies are made in post" (referring to the post-filming period), which is another way of saying that editing might be the most crucial step in producing a finished film. The technology makes amazing things possible, but a few tips on the artistry involved in the editing process makes amazing things probable.

Being a slash is a lot of work and responsibility, but it concentrates important tasks in the hands of the person most invested in getting the film finished, you.

KEY 4 — GEEK OUT

In your lifetime, filmmaking and film watching have been transformed. And as a direct result, you now need to be a geek.

Not all that many years ago, getting professional-looking images called for huge and expensive cameras that required great expertise to operate, and delicate film that was vulnerable to exposure and hugely expensive to develop. Editing required machinery that physically cut and spliced pieces of developed film together to get a finished product.

Now it's all 1s and 0s, baby. Ain't technology grand.

That's a bit of an exaggeration, as most studio films still require those big cameras and expensive film, but editing is now done digitally. The incredible thing is that you can produce films of professional quality using equipment that is easy to learn how to use, and relatively accessible. With the advent of digital video cameras and editing software like Mac's iMovie, the stuff you need to make a good movie is easily within reach.

We'll get more into the technical stuff later, so right now it's enough to say that in order to take advantage of what's out there you'll need access to a digital camcorder of some kind, and an Internet-connected computer equipped with film editing software and a bit of hard drive space. You need to master these gizmos, and be a social media and online web marketing ninja, as well.

We're not saying you have to own all the tech and film gear. Even though it's cheaper than a Panoflex 35mm, these digital gizmos are pricey. Don't sweat it. There are lots of ways to get access to a camera and a computer and the Internet, and most don't involve breaking and entering. There's no reason to get scared off by this key; geeking out is easier than you think.

KEY 5 — THE THREE-DAY SHOOT

Don't you love faculty work days? President's Day, Arbor Day, all those days that get you a three-day weekend? We have a suggestion. Instead of sleeping until two, make a movie.

The nice thing about choosing a five-minute film is that you can create a shooting schedule that fits neatly into a three-day weekend. It's not easy, and you're in for some long days, but you can capture your whole movie (or just about) in a Saturday, Sunday, and Monday. We'll give you the schedule that makes it possible.

The beauty of a three-day shoot is that it's easy to keep momentum. You can keep even the most overcommitted actor on task, and on set and on time, for three days. Friends that have volunteered to hold boom mikes, or bring sandwiches, or be an extra can stay focused for three days. You can handle the pressure of being in charge of everything for three days.

And if you keep focused and stay on schedule, you can get your whole movie in the can.

We understand that the three-day schedule may not work for everyone, particularly if you are making your movie as a part of a class that meets certain times during the week. That's okay, we've got some ideas for you, too.

KEY 6 — CUT OFF FOR CUTTING

You may be tempted to think that when you finish your three-day shoot — when it's a wrap — that you're done. Not even close. Now it's time for "post" — a time that is critical to determine the quality of your film. Editing may not have the sexiness and excitement of the set, but it's twice as fun. This is when you start to see the movie coming together. The storytelling happens in editing. Plus you don't have to worry about everybody showing up. It's just you and the computer.

Editing is so much fun, and so potentially time consuming as you tweak and fix and retouch, that there is a danger that this portion of the process may drag on and on. Editing can drag on long enough to put the whole project in danger.

To combat this we strongly suggest that you put yourself on a deadline. In the same way that the three-day shoot gives you structure and time pressure, editing on a deadline increases the likelihood of getting it done.

We suggest that you pick a festival or contest (see Chapter 12) that has a submission deadline that comes between four to six weeks after you wrap. Don't make deals with yourself. Don't think of this as a negotiable deadline. You must be finished by that day. And you will be.

Look forward to that day. You'll be a filmmaker.

So there are our recommendations. You'll probably follow about a third of them. That's cool. You'll make your own decisions, find a new way of doing things, make your own mistakes, and eventually wish you'd done what we'd suggested. That's all part of the deal.

Now, however, it's time for you to start making your movie.

You should start with an idea.

RESHOOT

Getting the film "in the can" is the most important thing of all. There are six keys to getting it finished:

- ▶ Keep your film short — five minutes is optimal.
- ▶ Write a script for your film before shooting.
- ▶ Do all the major jobs yourself — be a slash.
- ▶ Geek the tech of shooting, editing and distributing.
- ▶ Stick to a compact, three-day shooting schedule.
- ▶ Set a deadline to finish editing the project.

CHAPTER **2**

HONEY, I SHRUNK THE
CONCEPT

PICKING A SUBJECT FOR YOUR FILM: SHELVING *GODFATHER IV*

You're probably already tired of hearing this, and it's only the second chapter, but we're going to say it anyway. You're not really a filmmaker until you've pulled off your shorts — until the movie is in the can. So to speak. It is essential that you actually finish this first film, and getting there may mean changing your expectations about what your movie is going to look like.

It's time to go small.

Your filmmaking dreams were probably born in a dark theater, watching *Slum-dog Millionaire* or *Napoleon Dynamite* or *Gleaming the Cube*. It's only natural that when you think about making a film, you dream of a two-hour, full-length, feature film. Maybe you've imagined a sweeping four-hour epic depicting the history of contemporary dental practices, or a three-part film cycle set entirely in a hardware store in Dubuque starring Ethan Hawke. Indeed, you've probably seen so many Hollywood movies, that the storytelling structure of two-hour movies is already imbedded in your brainpan. More about structure later.

The epic studio "feature" is the big dream. Some day you'll get there, with the big house in the Hollywood Hills and lunch with Matt Damon and the whole deal. Put that up on a shelf for now. Not the trash, just a shelf. To get to the big dream you need to have a little dream first: a short film. And making a "short" is different from making a "feature" from the moment of conception — even the idea for a short film has to be different, or more to the point, smaller.

A feature is a gorgeous landscape hanging in the Louvre. A short is a postage stamp.

Lick it, stick it, and you're going places.

The first step in making a short film is coming up with a subject that is suitable for a five-minute movie. You've got to find an idea that fits.

BRAINSHOWERS

You don't need a whole brainstorm to come up with a subject for your short, a brainshower will do. In an ideal world (i.e. Steven Spielberg's office) there would be no limitations to what you could dream for your film. Pigs fly, cabbages duel with laser pistols and snappy dialogue, Keanu can act. However, when contemplating the story you want to tell in your first short, it is an unfortunate fact that you will have to keep some practicalities in mind. Namely, you have limited time and a limited budget.

At the brainshower stage, the most important practical consideration to keep in mind is time. Let's try to get a feel for just how long five minutes is in "movie time."

An Experiment

Go on Netflix and rent three movies. Watch them while keeping a close eye on a stopwatch. Start your watch when the credits (Directed by, etc.) finish and the narrative part of the movie begins. When the watch reads five minutes hit the pause button. How much of the story has been told? Now go back to your starting point and watch again, this time taking notes. Write down all that happens during the five minutes. This may take several runs through the clip, but the time is worth it.

When reviewing your notes from this experiment, observe the number of separate scenes presented in five minutes. You may be surprised, and even a bit depressed, by how little of the plot is presented in five minutes. Comfort yourself by reflecting on just how much information the director has communicated about the world of the film. What have you learned about the places and people in this movie in just five minutes? You've been told more than you think. You can say a lot about a little in five minutes.

Now that you have completed this exercise you probably have a better sense of just how compact a form you are working with. You're ready now to try to cook up a brainshower.

SUBJECT YOURSELF

Full-length films can take as their subject an individual's life, an era, the history of a family or a place, or a plot to destroy the earth. Short films can't really tackle such sweeping subjects very well. They can, however, effectively capture a moment in time. A short film is a snapshot, a glimpse, a fragment of a life.

You may already have a subject in mind for your short. If you do, you may want to think back to the stopwatch exercise. Compare your vision of your film with the reality of five minutes. Can you really tell your story in that period of time?

You will ultimately be in better shape if you choose a tiny subject or story and have the time to tell it completely, than if you try to shave down a larger tale to fit into a tiny frame. If your idea seems too big, hold on to it. It'll come in handy some day. Now it's time to look for another one. Get smaller.

Even if your idea survives scrutiny, don't be afraid to give it a little competition. Go ahead and complete the brainshowering exercises laid out later in the chapter. Come up with several ideas. If after all that, you still like your original idea, it's probably a good one.

When brainshowering for your film, consider the following list of generic subjects:

- ▶ An encounter
- ▶ A twist of fate
- ▶ A surprise
- ▶ An oddball
- ▶ A disruption
- ▶ A dream

A note on ideas: In reading the list of suggested subjects above, an idea may have popped into your head. Write it down! Make sure you keep a notebook handy while you are reading (or walking, or napping, or showering), and if an idea hits you, drop this book like a hot rock and scribble like a maniac. (The authors suggest that you keep several copies of this book handy in case one is damaged in this process.)

If you are still holding this book after reading through our list of suggested subjects, you may need a jumpstart. Try one or both of the following exercises. It is important at this phase not to edit yourself. Let ideas flow, even if you are sure that they are terrible. Lots of terrible ideas become movies. A few of them are even good.

Jumpstart Exercise 1: Blab!

The blank screen or blank page is the most depressing thing in the world to a writer — student and professional alike. It's important to break the ice, to get rolling even if it is complete nonsense. Nonsense is better than blank. Consider using that stopwatch you had with you while watching movies. Give yourself ten minutes.

Ready. Set. Blab.

Just start writing. Anything. It could be a to-do list. It could be a letter to a favorite pet, anything, just get the pen or cursor moving across the page.

Blab away to yourself until you feel ready to start writing about your movie idea. Trick yourself. Go from complaining about how boring Algebra is to your vision for a film without pausing to worry about it. The important thing in this exercise is to never stop writing, even if it is nonsense. You may churn out several ideas; keep writing. Don't edit, judge or even think. If it pops into your head, put it on the page.

Blab away! It could lead to brilliance.

Jumpstart Exercise 2: Define the Problem

Choose one or more of the generic subjects suggested in our list earlier in this chapter. Write the subject as a heading to the page. Now write a definition of that word. It doesn't have to be the dictionary definition. The definition should be your own interpretation of the word.

Next, give three examples of the word you have defined. These examples could be from your imagination, or from "real life." Write down: "An example of _____ (your generic subject) is _____ ." As always at this stage, it is important to put these examples down without thinking about them very much. Fill in the blanks as if you were taking a Biology test with 100 questions and only a few minutes left in the period.

Once you've completed these exercises, you may have generated a few ideas, but there is no reason to stop there. There are several more avenues to a great idea for a short.

THE REAL WORLD

We've all seen those movies that boast that they are "based on a true story." Why do the producers choose to tell us that? Because audiences like it. Audiences like to relax and believe what they see. "True" stories reassure an audience that what is coming won't be fake or silly or, worst of all, cliché — something based on stereotypes we've all seen a million times.

Use your own "true stories" when brainshowering. Do you have an experience that's unique? What have you seen or done that makes you stand out in the crowd? Know somebody unusual? Been somewhere cool? Peeked behind the scenes where us regular folks never get to go?

Creating stories based on personal experience is a great way to ensure that your script will be unique and truthful, and therefore interesting to an audience.

BE ADAPTABLE

Other than winning the Academy Award for Best Picture, what do *Chicago*, *The Silence of the Lambs*, *Forrest Gump*, *Lord of the Rings: Return of the King*, and *A Beautiful Mind* have in common? All are adaptations. An adaptation is a movie script that is based on another work — a play (*Chicago*), a novel (*Forrest Gump*), or a non-fiction book (*A Beautiful Mind*). In fact, in the last ten years the majority of Oscar winners and top-grossing films were adaptations.

Adaptations can be extremely faithful, sticking close to the style and events of the original "source material," or they can take liberties, make changes, and shift emphasis. Many have noted that the *Harry Potter* movies have been very faithful to the original novels, taking lines of dialogue directly from the book. On the other hand, Francis Ford Coppola's famous film *Apocalypse Now* is an example of a film "loosely based on" or "inspired by" another work. Set during the Vietnam War in the 1960s, *Apocalypse Now* is adapted from the novella *Heart of Darkness* written by Joseph Conrad in the 1890s.

If you still aren't satisfied with a subject for your film, consider an adaptation.

Because you are making a short, in all likelihood *War and Peace* would be a poor choice of source material for your adaptation (break this rule). Rather, you might consider looking at shorter forms as the basis for your script. How about a great song, or a poem you love?

The following will sound dorky, but try to keep an open mind. We also suggest that you consider myths, legends, folktales, and children's stories as sources of adaptation. This technique can be particularly funny if you decide to work in a "loosely based on" mode. What happens to "The Frog Prince" when you set it in a school cafeteria?

A note on adaptation: If you do decide to adapt, remember that you are borrowing from a fellow writer. If you follow that writer's work too closely you may be infringing on his or her copyright (another good reason to use fairy tales — no copyright). If you have any questions about copyright, you may want to check with a teacher or adult. If you intend to submit your movie to festivals, it's important to be careful.

CULLING THE HERD

At this point you probably have subject ideas out the wazoo. You've got the ideas you've had long before you ever picked up this book, you've got your Blabbing and your Definitions, you've got your personal experiences, and you've got your adaptations.

You may know instantly upon looking at your notebook which idea you want to live with for the next few months. The hair stands up on the back of your neck when you think about it, or you let out a snorting laugh in the middle of the library when you consider the possibilities. These are good signs that you have found your subject.

If you are struggling with the decision, imagine screening the movie for your closest friends and family. What film moves them, amuses them, challenges them the most? What idea makes your best friend laugh the hardest? What idea will make your favorite teacher the most proud?

Pick that and run with it.

GET INTO TREATMENT

Now that you have a subject, the next step should be a "Treatment." A treatment is a prose (essay) precursor or preview of your script. This is a continuation of the brainshowering process in which you get the bare bones of the story on paper. In simple language, tell the story of your movie. Say a word or two about each of the major characters as they appear: age, distinguishing physical or psychological features. Tell your reader about the major events or incidents of the movie. Don't try to get too fancy. Keep it simple and straightforward: what happens, and then what happens after that.

TREATMENT, "DETENTION DEFICIT":
A girl finds herself in detention, but she is not sure why. She recounts the day's events and all the things that she did that could have gotten her in trouble. She remembers another kid who got in trouble and did not make it to see the light of day. She begins to plan her elaborate escape when the teacher falls asleep. She sees her chance and makes a run for it, but from what?

For a five-minute short, a treatment should be half a page or less. It could simply be a paragraph or even just a couple of sentences. (At this stage it is important to get into the habit of translating your ideas to the page before you commit them to film.) If you find the treatment growing longer than that, creeping to a full page or longer, it may be a sign that your story is too ambitious.

If this is difficult, consider recruiting a friend (who can write fast) or using a tape recorder. Ask your friend to take notes while you tell him or her the story of your movie, or try narrating the story into the tape recorder. Use these notes as the outline for your treatment. Or you could simply transcribe your recording. Instant treatment.

This is an important step and it will make writing the actual script much easier.

PUT IT TO BED

Now that you have your treatment, put it away for a couple of days, maybe a weekend. When you come back to it, does it still make you smile? Does the hair on the back of your neck still do that thing? You may not think it was as brilliant as when you first wrote it, but a spark needs to still be there. You are going to be pouring a lot of time and effort into this thing. If you don't still like it, now is the time to turn back and start over.

Don't move on to the process described in the next chapter until you've got a treatment you still like a few days later.

If you get that treatment out of bed and you can't wait to show it to your friends and family, can't wait for that movie to be up on the screen, it's time to move on to the next chapter.

GETTING IT PAST THE CENSORS

We think that you should make the movie you want to make, in your own voice, reflecting the truth as you see it. You should protect the integrity of your artistic vision.

Ideally.

In reality, there are some practical considerations to keep in mind when choosing subject matter for (and later writing) your film. If you are interested in gaining the support, financial or logistical, of adults (teachers or parents, mostly, but also anyone else who might see the script), you might want to consider avoiding certain subjects. If you want your movie shown at school, or in any academic setting, consider avoiding the following in your film:

▶ *Swearing*

▶ *Smoking*

▶ *Use of drugs or alcohol/house parties*

▶ *Graphic violence*

▶ *Graphic sex*

▶ *Teen suicide*

▶ *School violence*

What fun is that? We're not saying you have to avoid all these things, just know what the practical consequences of using them are. Aunt Sally isn't going to buy you sound equipment for a movie where folks talk like Lil' Wayne. The principal of your school isn't going to screen a movie with excessive violence. Don't be surprised when adults roll up the red carpet.

RESHOOT

Keep it small and you'll get it finished. This starts with the concept.

▶ Watch just five minutes of feature films to get a feel.

▶ Choose a tiny subject, a snapshot.

▶ Use freewriting to kick off the writing process — don't edit!

▶ Consider an adaptation or a true story.

▶ Write a treatment, a short prose synopsis of the story.

CHAPTER 3

SCREENPLAY
THE EVERY OTHER DAILY GRIND

WHY YOU SCRIPT

Now it's time to write the script. Don't worry, it'll all be over in three weeks.

We understand that you may be bumming at the notion of writing a script. After all, when you think about making movies, you think about being behind the camera, actors doing their thing, lights glaring down. You probably don't picture sitting at a computer. The bad news is that in reality, you'll spend many more hours at the computer (for both writing and editing) than you will behind the camera. Sorry about that. Wish we could tell you different. In addition, writing is probably the part of the process that feels the most like a homework assignment.

The good news is that just twenty-one days from the time you start, you'll be sitting down with a group of friends to have a read-through of your screenplay. When that reading is done, you're a screenwriter — a major component of slashdom — and you're much closer to being a filmmaker.

Don't be tempted to skip this step.

We know you're thinking about it. Admit it. You are thinking to yourself, I've got a concept, maybe even a treatment. *We can make the rest up as we go along. It'll be spontaneous. Actors can make up their lines. Bing, bang, boom. It'll be cool.*

It'll also be amateurish. A home video.

The script guides what happens on the set.

Having a script is the factor that will separate your film from the crowd of teen-made flicks. How? Because writing a script improves the work on the set for both creative and practical reasons. From a creative standpoint, the writing process forces you to clarify your idea, mostly by streamlining. Writing forces you to be specific and to work out problems that are probably a bit fuzzy in your head. The result of writing is a much clearer and simpler story.

From a practicality standpoint, the screenplay is important because it allows you and your production team to prepare thoroughly for the shoot. Once on location, the script helps everyone on the set, literally, to be "on the same page." It will save you lots of time to hand out scripts rather than explaining to every person on the set what you want in a particular shot. Make sure that when it comes time to be on the set that the producer (you) has lots of extra copies in a box in a prominent place.

Most kids just don't have the discipline to sit down and grind it out, and the films suffer. But you'll have the focus, because we have a plan that will get your script done in just three weeks.

BUT BEFORE YOU START...

Before plowing ahead, think back for a moment. Remember where you found this book? Whether it was at a bookstore or the local public library, this little gem was probably sharing shelf-space with a number of honest-to-goodness screenplays. Go back to that place, and pick up one of those beauties. It doesn't really matter which one. Now surf on over to Netflix and pick out the DVD of that same movie.

Screen the movie with the screenplay open on your lap. Despite your natural inclination, try to give the bulk of your attention to the page, glancing up as you go to catch the visual.

This exercise will do a couple of good things for you. First, it familiarizes you with the screenplay format (more on that in a minute). It's actually much simpler than it looks. Second, you'll get a feel for the pace of the screenplay. Pay particular attention to the stage directions, those sections of the script that describe what happens on screen. We think you'll notice that these directions are pretty spare — lean — pared down — economical — you get it.

In the process you may also notice places where the screenplay and the film are different. Can you imagine why this may have happened? Keep these speculations in the back of your mind — the same issues may arise in your own film.

SCREENPLAY FORMAT

The screenplay format is practical because it lays things out in a wide-open, readable format that separates the information for visuals (stage direction) from dialogue. The proper format also has a nifty feature: each page of screenplay roughly equals one minute of screen time. Ergo: five minutes = five pages.

We're just talking about five short pages here. You've written History papers twice as long as that.

There is some variation in screenplay format, but for our purposes, the simplest format is the best. We recommend that you concern yourself with only three things: slug lines, stage directions, and dialogue.

A NOTE ON SCREENWRITING SOFTWARE

There are lots of screenwriting software packages on the market that will format your screenplay for you. Some actually claim to help you write your story! In our opinion, a program called "Final Draft" is the best of the bunch. This program will speed your writing along by formatting automatically — it even remembers character names and fills them in for you.

The program has some other nifty advanced features for taking notes on your screenplay, and preparing the finished piece for production. The downside is that this program is somewhat pricey — even with the available student discounts, the software will cost over $100. How valuable is your time? We suggest you avoid the creepy, machine-writes-your-screenplay programs altogether. Ever seen *2001: A Space Odyssey*?

If you'd rather save the money to upgrade your mic, check to see if your word processing program offers a screenplay template. Mac's Pages offers a reasonably good one, and a student software bundle may be less expensive than a full screenwriting rig. If a template is not available, setting up the screenplay format is easy in most widely available word processing software. In Microsoft Word, for example, try creating two "styles" — one for directions and one for dialogue. That should be enough.

STAGE DIRECTIONS

You'll see that most of the words in a screenplay are in the blocks of stage directions. There's a reason for this. Film is a visual medium (duh) and these are the portions of the script that describe what the viewer sees. It is important here for the screenwriter to think in pictures, and to transcribe those pictures clearly. Make sure that you include those essential details that give the image its distinctive qualities. Write what you see.

But not *everything* that you see. While it's crucial that you communicate what the viewer sees in the shot, even to provide some detail, it's easy to overdo it. Keep your descriptions direct and clear. Use simple sentences. Long tangled sentences are your enemy. Eschew them. Keep it short. Be direct. Less is more. Okay, you get it.

Notice that stage directions run from margin to margin without indentation and are single spaced.

SLUG LINES

No, slug lines are not the shiny/nasty trails that snails leave behind. They are titles that introduce scenes or sequences. They carry simple information about location and time of day. They serve as little dividers between scenes or series of shots. These dividers will be useful when you are setting up your shooting schedule.

Notice that the slug lines are in all capital letters, but are not tabbed or indented. They can be in the same "style" as your stage directions. INT. stands for interior (inside) and EXT. stands for exterior (outside). The location is then named. No reason to get too cute here, but do make sure that the crew will all know quickly where they are headed. Then indicate DAY or NIGHT. This is important info to the techies, with obvious impact on camera and lighting.

Putting in a slug line is a little like starting a new paragraph in an essay. If there is a significant shift in location or scene, throw in a slug line. You don't, however, need a new slug line for every single shot. A conversation between two characters might require a number of different shots, but until they get up and go outside, or get in a car, or suddenly detonate, no new slug line is required. If a series of shots seems to hang together as a unit, don't bother separating them all with slug lines.

In general, where to put in slug lines is more an art than a science. You'll get the hang of it very quickly, so don't sweat it too much.

DIALOGUE

You may have noticed that in the screenplay format, stage directions roam far and wide, from margin to margin, unencumbered and free, whereas the poor dialogue is squeezed into the center of the page. Shackled between tabs set in one inch from both the left and right margins, dialogue is pinched into the center of the page. Do you sense a value judgment here?

Some might say that film is a visual medium (duh, again) and therefore the story-telling should happen mostly through what the audience sees (stage directions) and not through what the characters say (dialogue). This value of picture over words is reflected in the format. (An interesting note: The format for stage plays is the exact opposite of screenplay format — the dialogue goes from margin to margin, and stage directions are crunched in the center — language being more important than visuals in a play.)

This doesn't necessarily mean that your characters should only speak in Schwartzeneggerian grunts and monosyllables. It doesn't mean that we shouldn't hear your characters speak their minds. Indeed, the audience wants to know the people you create. When they speak, in grunts or in paragraphs, they should speak distinctively. Every character should have his or her unique voice.

When you are done writing, you should be able to cover the character's name in the script and still know exactly who it is that is speaking, based on what they say and how they say it.

Remember that you have only five minutes. If your characters are going to talk a lot, it had better be really interesting talking. There is no time to talk about what happened before (also known as exposition − it's deadly in a short) and there is no time to talk about things the audience has also seen. If you avoid dialogue that is expository (about the "backstory" or past) or redundant (telling about something we already saw), you've won half the dialogue battle. Give your characters distinctive voices, speech patterns, verbal tics, expressions, humor, vocabulary − and you'll master the art of dialogue.

The following is an excerpt from one of our student-written scripts in the proper format.

```
INT. CLASSROOM − DAY

High school students arrayed in a semi-circle
surround a teacher, MR. REOUS, at the blackboard.
He drones.

                    REOUS
          ...the metaphor explores the
          line between life and death,
          sentience and absence, thinking
          and unthinking. The metaphor...

SEBASTIAN tumbles in, backpack flopping over, almost
pulling him down. He finds a seat.

                    REOUS
          Eight minutes late. Pretty
          good for you.
```

REOUS goes back to his lecture, exploring
metaphors. SEBASTIAN looks over to get his props
from his neighbors VIN and VAN. He is surprised
to see that both boys are wearing the exact same
Abercrombie T-shirt. SEBASTIAN smirks and leans
over to hassle them.

> SEBASTIAN
>
> Nice.

VIN and VAN hardly react. They simply turn and
stare at him blankly. This reaction unnerves
SEBASTIAN. He returns his attention to the teacher.

EXT. BREEZEWAY — DAY

SEBASTIAN exits his class right behind VIN and
VAN. They distract him just enough that he
almost collides with MANDY, his girlfriend who
is cute and blonde, intelligent but missing a
bit of common sense, coming up to him and giving
him a big bear hug.

> MANDY
>
> Sebastian! I haven't seen you
> in so long!

> SEBASTIAN
>
> Yeah, Friday till Monday.
> Eternity.

OVER MANDY's shoulder SEBASTIAN notices a
cluster of three kids wearing the Vin and Van
T-shirt, all the people standing in poses and
moving as if they were pictures in a catalogue.

THE STORY, A COUPLE IDEAS

Having been through the brainshowering process, you've already done a fair amount of thinking about story, or plot. You may have even written a treatment, which will make the scripting process a piece of cake.

START LATE

As you sit down to start writing, it's a good time to remember, yet again, that we're only talking five minutes here — five (or six or seven) measly pages. Therefore you want to start your script as late as possible. A late start is key. Now this doesn't mean waiting up past Letterman before you sit down at the computer (though the teens we've worked with never seem to start writing before midnight). By starting late, we mean choosing the last possible moment to begin telling your story. This serves to compress your movie and make it more interesting.

Looking at your treatment, what is the last second in the story where you could begin without hopelessly confusing your audience? Hopeless confusion is bad. A little confusion, on the other hand....

In our opinion, a little confusion on the part of the audience can actually be a good thing. If your audience has to work a little bit to catch up with what is going on, then they are likely to become engaged in the film.

Start late, and don't be afraid of asking your audience to hustle a little bit to keep up. You've got to move fast, after all.

STAYING AHEAD OF THE CROWD: REVERSALS

Movie audiences hate, more than anything, to be bored. And most audiences are filled with people who have seen thousands of movies. The most frequent causes of audience boredom are stock characters or situations. "Stock" means stereotypical, familiar, or overused.

Nowhere do you find more overused and stereotyped characters than in movies about teens. You know what we're talking about, so we won't even mention them here (that would make me a nerd, or maybe a jock, or a cheerleader, or a Goth) — avoid these like open manhole covers. Our guess is that you view your fellow teens as being complex, multi-hued, layered; the way most human beings are. Shouldn't they appear that way in your film?

To keep the audience from getting bored, it's very important to stay ahead of them. If your audience anticipates where your story is headed, they turn off quicker than your mom's reading light at 11. Don't be predictable, either with character, or with plot. Zag when they expect you to play Monopoly. Don't go in the direction that your audience anticipates. We call these moments, when you dodge audience expectation, reversals. A reversal can be subtle or outrageous. A reversal is simply the moment when you shift the story in a way the audience didn't see coming. A reversal can be a character acting in a way that turns "stock" on its head. A reversal can come from plot or character.

Reversals look like twists and turns. But in reality, reversals keep your audience right with you.

Exercise: Look at your treatment and identify the reversals. Where are the moments in your story that you give the audience the slip, give them something different from what they might expect? There should be at least one. If you have very few or none, can you devise a way to add an element of surprise, the unique, the unexpected? A reversal or two?

This suggestion, like any other, should be taken in balance. Don't go wacky just to stay ahead of the audience. Your piece may be dramatic in ways that makes being unpredictable difficult; try instead to be truthful. So few movies about teens are, that truth, in and of itself, will be a surprise.

Okay. The Time Has Come. Let's face the keyboard.

THE WRITING PROCESS: THREE WEEKS LATER

How do they do it, these writers? These magicians who seem to pull books and screenplays out of the air? Take it from us, there is absolutely, positively nothing magical about it. As we write this book, we'd really rather be watching sports. But we know that won't cut it. We want to get it done.

To pull it all off, it's all about making a schedule, sticking to it, and grinding it out. You should make a writing schedule. We suggest a simple schedule of writing half a page every other day — and by doing this you can finish the first draft of your script in only three weeks.

We acknowledge that no one schedule works for all writers. There are almost as many writing processes as there are scribblers. Inspiration can come all at once or it can come very gradually, in little bits and pieces. You'll find a way of writing that works for you. We've known writers that have to lock themselves away in a cabin with no telephone to work. We also know writers that work in front of the

TV. You may find that you are a writer that needs at least four hours of time to get anything done, so you are going to have to set aside time on the weekends, or do your writing in the summer. Some writers need only a small window of thirty to forty-five minutes to get something down. You may already know what is comfortable for you, or you may have to experiment a bit.

YOUR WRITING CALENDAR

Once you know how you work best, set up a timetable for yourself, and if you can write in brief chunks — write it on your class schedule, during free periods or study halls. Three per week would be ideal. Think of it as signing up for an elective class three periods a week. Write it into your schedule. Where there are blank spaces, write "screenwriting."

If you need longer stretches, schedule an hour and a half to two-hour sessions on three successive Saturdays or Sundays. Write it on a calendar somewhere you'll see it, and don't double-book yourself. If you can, put yourself down for the afternoon, so you won't sleep through your writing time. Don't schedule work. Don't run errands.

Keep to the schedule once you set it up. You can even set up a system of rewards for yourself. Buy a box of Ding-Dongs (or Snoballs or whatever junk food nightmare is closest to your heart) and allow yourself to eat them only after a writing session. Your screenwriting Skittles. Your creative Co-Co Puffs. Your inspiration ice cream.

Think of it this way: if you can manage to write just a bit more than half a page, three days a week or a touch more than a page and a half each Saturday, you can have a first draft of your script finished in just three weeks!

SCHEDULE A READING

As the final component of your writing calendar, you should schedule a reading of the first draft of the screenplay. Put it on your calendar the Monday or Tuesday after you are scheduled to finish the script. This is your deadline, gives you something solid to shoot for, and ensures you that you will get some feedback on your script before going ahead with the project.

Our next suggestion will sound insane, but you need to think seriously about it. The first thing you should write, even before your first line of stage directions (movies usually start with the line FADE IN ON) — a poster advertising the reading of the script. Print out ten copies and post them in various places.

Think you'll back out now? The poster, staring you in the face for three weeks, will motivate you like nothing else. Imagine showing up at the reading with nothing to present.

It's all about getting it done.

SCREENWRITING UNPLUGGED

If it weren't for the fabulous technology now widely available, we wouldn't be writing this book. Kids wouldn't be making movies all over the place. Technology is great.

Except when you're writing.

When you are writing your screenplay, you may wish at times that you could transport yourself back to the days of the typewriter. The big problem is that the machine that serves as your word processor is now also a video game player, email center, jukebox, movie theatre, telephone, social networking portal and more.

When you are writing, do your best to keep all these features off. Surf the Internet only after you're done. Turn IM off and keep Facebook closed. While you're at it, turn off your cell phone and tell your mom to hold your calls.

DON'T INTERROGATE THE DRAFT

Okay, you're off and running. You're typing away; the creativity is flowing; you're getting pretty close to your half page for the day. You maybe even start composing your Academy Award acceptance speech in your head. It's brilliant.

You pause to read back over what you've done, when suddenly some part of your subconscious starts screaming at you:

I HATE IT! IT SUCKS! THIS IS HORRIBLE! I CAN'T POSSIBLY SHOW THIS TO ANY-ONE, MUCH LESS FILM IT!

Remain calm. This is perfectly normal.

Even professional writers go through this roller-coaster during the creative process. There will be times when you have doubt about what you are doing. It is essential that you know that these feelings are an inevitable part of the creative process and you KEEP WRITING!

Don't judge this early writing too harshly, particularly as it emerges in the first draft. Your screenplay, your whole film, is emerging and is a bit delicate and vulnerable. Don't squish it. Be tolerant of a piece that is not perfect, and keep writing.

If you demand that your first draft be perfect, exactly like you dreamed it would be, you will never finish the screenplay, and you will never make a great movie. In order to pull off your shorts, you have got to be patient with yourself, tell that "IT SUCKS" voice to leave you alone, and keep writing.

Note: Self-criticism in the early stages of writing can be debilitating. These bouts of self-criticism usually happen as you go back and reread a previous day's work. If you find that this happens consistently, don't go back and reread. Only plow ahead. Don't stop to reread until the screenplay is finished. This will keep your forward momentum going.

Stick to your writing schedule, keep ahead of your audience, and don't interrogate your first draft, and in three weeks, you've got a script.

Just in time for that reading you've been advertising all over the place.

READINGS: GETTING SOMETHING FOR NOTHING

LISTEN CAREFULLY

The most important thing to do at a reading is to listen and take notes. The only thing the audience should hear from you is the scratch of your pencil on your notebook. Don't act in the reading, don't explain what you intended, listen. If you have to speak, all of your sentences should end in a question mark.

This will not be easy. Because you wrote it, you know exactly how all the lines should sound, so you'll naturally want to say them. But if you are concentrating on acting your part, you can't listen effectively. It's impossible to do both. Let others do the acting.

Besides, the reading is a great opportunity to pre-audition some actors. Don't be shy about asking people to read for you. (This is a good chance to practice asking people for help. Get used to it.) You'll be surprised how interested people will be. Go ahead and invite people, actors, whoever you have been picturing in the movie when you were writing, to come read. It's okay to ask friends that aren't necessarily actors. It's okay to have people read more than one role.

Don't forget to get someone to read the stage directions.

Make sure to issue personal invitations to friends and teachers whose opinion you trust to come to the reading. Making a personal request can make a difference. Don't shy away from opinionated people.

You might even consider springing for some pizza.

QUIZ SHOW

Before the reading, pick one of your actors, maybe the stage directions reader. Ask him or her to announce that there will be an opportunity for the audience to give the writer some feedback at the end. Also hand this person a card with preprinted questions on it. When the reading is over, ask this person to serve as moderator. People will feel much more comfortable giving feedback if they are asked by someone other than the writer.

Consider starting with the following questions:
    1) What about this story engaged you? (enjoy this one)
    2) Did anything confuse you? Throw you? Cause you to drop out of the story?
    3) What is the central conflict of the story?
    4) Ask questions specific to your script. (What are you most worried about the audience getting?)

As the feedback comes in, especially if people don't get it or are confused, you'll feel a powerful impulse to explain what you meant. Resist.

The purpose of the reading is for you to learn if the audience is hearing what you are saying, based on what is written. If you have to explain, then they aren't getting it. You need to be more clear. Keep your mouth shut! Say it in your script. Your audience is telling you what you need to know. If you have to explain, then you're not doing your job as a writer. It is absolutely critical that you take advantage of this time to listen and take notes.

Ask your moderator to move along pretty quickly. Lots of times people giving feedback will get into hearing themselves talk. There may even be some wannabe-but-never-pull-them-off types in your audience that know exactly what you should do. Take notes. If somebody is a real jerk, write "real jerk" in your notes. This is very empowering. Don't let it go longer than 20 minutes. If you go past that, just say "I've got a lot to think about here. I think this is enough for today."

The Making Of

Got access to a camera? Why not shoot the reading? Set the camera on a tripod and get a wide shot of the whole cast. Just turn the camera on and let it roll. Don't let it distract you from listening. Turn it on, turn it off. You may like having this record to refer to at a later point during the rewrite. You may also want to publish this video once the project is complete, in order to fill out your channel on video sharing sites (more on this in Chapter 13).

DO OVER

After all five questions have been posed, and the feedback has been expressed, have the actors read it again. It's only five or so minutes long, after all. This time listen with the audience feedback in mind. Do some of the things make sense to you? Do you hear them also? Put a star in your notebook next to those entries.

When the reading is over, review your notes. Then throw them away. Don't be tempted to go home and make revisions. You've done more than enough for one day. You're probably exhausted. Get some sleep.

The next day go back to your notebook and try to remember two or three notes from the reading. Only write down things that really struck you, resonated with you. If someone gave you some feedback and to yourself you said "Yes!" or began nodding your head uncontrollably, put those notes back in your notebook. Remind yourself that this is your screenplay. Unless the feedback confirms something that you already thought or suspected, maybe even at a subconscious level, forget it.

It's your story. Let other people help you figure out what you already knew.

REVISION: HELLO OLD FRIEND

We know it's hard, after struggling for three weeks to get a draft of the screenplay, to imagine that you aren't finished. Perhaps the reading helped a bit. It is worth the trouble to go back and address some of the ideas that came out of the reading. Give yourself another week of writing sessions for rewrites. We know we said three weeks — consider this a revision.

Give yourself the opportunity to improve the screenplay, but don't fall into the trap of endlessly rewriting to make the script perfect. A week is enough.

And once you're done, you're done. Get committed to this script. This is what you will shoot, hickies and all. Shoot this script exactly as it is.

OVERTIME

Help, my screenplay is ten pages long! (Or eight, or even six.)

This is not such a huge deal. Ever play Jenga?

It's a natural tendency in the first draft of a screenplay to overwrite. By overwriting, we mean that you will include information that the audience doesn't need or gets elsewhere. It is very important that you be a bit ruthless with your writing. Get out the red pen and put it on your desk.

At this point, part of your writer's mind will whimper and beg you to preserve every precious word. This part of your mind will whine about how hard you worked, how funny everything is, how important for character development every single line is.

Tell that weenie to shut up, and take the cap off the pen.

Now to our Jenga metaphor. In the game, players alternate pushing wooden blocks out of a wooden tower. The player who causes the tower to collapse, loses. This is like cutting. The game here is to remove every single word you can without the story collapsing.

Go through your script and ask of every shot, every line of dialogue, every word: does it have to be there? Can the audience understand the story without it? If the answer is yes, apply the red. Keep this up until you get under five (or six) pages.

We know there will be some painful moments in this process. Some great lines and scenes will be lost. You will thank yourself in the long run, because you've greatly increased the probability that your film will get done. You are doing the other parts of your slash a favor here. Your producer/director/editor selves will thank you for making their lives so much easier by showing a bit of discipline.

Now print it out again.

Check it out. You wrote a movie.

RESHOOT
Don't be tempted to skip scripting. It only takes three weeks.

- ▶ Schedule your writing times, stick to it.
- ▶ Familiarize yourself with screenplay format: watch and read simultaneously.
- ▶ Start late and use reversals.
- ▶ Announce a reading before you even start writing.
- ▶ Don't be critical of the first draft.
- ▶ Listen carefully (and be quiet) at the reading, then revise.
- ▶ Cut ruthlessly until it's short.

CHAPTER **4**

THE
PRODUCERS

YOU'RE NOT A CHEESEBALL

Okay, now that the script is finished, it's time to switch hats. Time to enter another realm of slashdom. Time to be the producer. What is your picture of a film producer? Cigar-chomping, sunglasses-inside-sporting, silk-shirt-wearing sleezebag?

Well, yes. But not always.

So what is it that a producer actually does?

In reality, the producer is the driving force behind the creation of the film. The producer is the practical one, the one that manages all the details, solves all the problems, so the art can happen. It is in this role that you will lay the groundwork for the shoot. You'll assemble a crew, create a shooting schedule, scout a location, wrangle props, costumes and other production elements, and even arrange for food.

This job will challenge your organizational and social skills, but it can also be a great deal of fun. You'll master the fine art of asking favors, mooching, solving problems, begging, working out differences of opinion, and getting things at a discount. You'll be the leader of a band of crazy filmmakers. That's your job as producer.

And it's always good to remember this: Who is it that walks to the podium and picks up the Oscar for the best picture? The producer.

YOUR PEEPS

As producer the very most important thing you will do is pick good people to work with you. The second most important thing you'll do is to get them to all show up.

In this process, you're going to be cashing in a ton of karma. You'll be asking a lot of people to put in a lot of hours, essentially to serve your artistic vision and interest. They'll have a great time and learn a lot, but you need to constantly keep in mind that you cannot do this without them, and that they are doing the work essentially out of the goodness of their hearts. Anything that you can do in the process to thank, praise, feed, and otherwise enrich the experience for your cast and crew will help your movie.

Therefore, be nice to your cast and crew at all times, starting from the moment when you approach them to ask for help. Be nice to them even when they screw up. Even when you are running out of time and it starts to rain. Even when they break the equipment. Always be nice to them. And you also need to feed them. We'll remind you of this again later.

THE SUPERFRIENDS

When it comes to assembling a crew, you will have four key people that will be with you, giving their time, for virtually the whole shoot. These are the Associate Producer, the Assistant Director, the Camera Operator, and the Sound Engineer. These are your Superfriends. These are the people you are going to be asking to give up a vacation to be a part of your project. These are the people you have to depend on to be there, on time, every day. That should tell you something about the kind of people you want to be talking to.

Most slashes look naturally to draw these four key people from their circle of friends. It's not a bad idea. Presumably, your friends are people you can depend on, people that will back you up and help you out.

But the problem with friends is, well, they're your friends. Are they the people you are the most productive with? The important question to ask is, can I have a good time with my friends and still get the work done? Can you study effectively with your friends? If you do decide to go with your closest buddies, make sure to try to fit them into roles that best suit their personalities, according to the descriptions to follow.

You might also consider choosing people that you know would fit well into the roles listed below even if they aren't your best friends. It's not a terrible thing to pick people that maybe don't know you as well. They might be more likely to take you seriously. You are going to have to give a lot of directions, a lot of orders, and the people on your crew are going to need to carry those out. It's very important to pick people that you will work with effectively and efficiently. There'll be time on the set to laugh and have a good time, but not much.

Your film will be best served if you look around yourself — your school, your neighborhood, your circle of friends — and without taking friendship into consideration, ask yourself "who would be the best at this?"

RAISE YOUR HAND

This actually might be a good time to get adults involved. Who is the teacher/counselor/administrator whose opinion you value most? Consider going to that person with your job descriptions and asking for recommendations. Who does that person think would be a good fit with the job and with you?

Give him or her a copy of the script and ask for responses while you're at it.

This meeting will serve a couple of purposes. You might get some names, some ideas, some feedback from someone you respect, but you are also recruiting someone who might be able to help you down the line. After all this person is a grown up, with keys and access to equipment, able to vouch for you with other adults. By asking an opinion and showing the script, you probably just sucked this person into being the unofficial faculty sponsor of your production. And they never even had time to say they're too busy.

SUPERFRIENDS: PERSONALITY PROFILES AND JOB DESCRIPTIONS

Below is a checklist of traits that serve these positions well. Of course the person you pick probably doesn't have all of these traits. You're not looking for a computer, you're looking for help.

Associate Producer

▸ organized
▸ good at resolving conflicts
▸ a problem solver
▸ lots of energy
▸ positive outlook
▸ "no worries"
▸ best class: math/science

Job Description: responsible for assisting the slash in the preproduction elements of casting, location scouting, prop and costume wrangling, etc. On the set this person essentially becomes the producer, solving logistical and practical problems that arise when the slash is in director mode. This person is the fireman on the set, putting out fires as they crop up.

Assistant Director
▶ calm under fire
▶ leader without being bossy
▶ no power trip/ no bull
▶ no nonsense
▶ would be elected captain by the crew
▶ best class: history/social studies

Job Description: Assists the director in the preproduction casting and rehearsal process. During filming, the boss of the set. Directs technical folks, mobilizes all personnel to get the shot the director wants. The slash decides what she wants; it's up to the AD to "make it so." A benevolent despot.

Camera Operator

▶ artistic

▶ enjoys still photography

▶ good at graphic arts/web design

▶ understands composition

▶ can name five famous visual artists

▶ collaborative; takes direction well

▶ good physical endurance

▶ best class: art/computer science

Job Description: the eye in the camera. The person who frames the shot under the advice of the director, and pushes the red button. Should be very familiar with all operations of the camera.

Note: This job is only necessary if you have a monitor, which we highly recommend. If you can't have a monitor, then it probably doesn't make a lot of sense to have a camera operator. You'll just be tripping over one another trying to get a look into the camera.

Sound Engineer

- ▶ has a diverse and well-stocked iPod
- ▶ insists on high quality headphones, doesn't settle for earbuds
- ▶ plays the electric guitar
- ▶ at home with wires and plugs
- ▶ precise, on the ball, exact
- ▶ likes puzzles
- ▶ best class: shop or jazz orchestra

Job Description: Responsible to coordinate with the camera operator in order to get the best sound possible. Must untangle and keep connected miles of wires and equipment.

REALLY GOOD BUT NOT QUITE SUPER FRIENDS

The four people listed above aren't the only folks you're going to have to sweet talk into being on your crew. You also need a platoon of techies and helpers who will set up lights, wrap cables, carry boxes, pick up the lunch, find a goat — whatever you need to get done.

An ideal laundry list of other crew members would look like this:

▸ 2 "Gaffers" — in charge of electrical things like lights, work closely with camera operator and director.

▸ 2 "Grips" — helps with all gear from tripods to sound cables, work closely with camera operator and sound engineer.

▸ 2 "PAs" — aka Production Assistants, Associate Producer/Assistant Director's helpers: some might be tempted to call them gophers, but you won't because they're too important — in charge of getting and fixing and helping in whatever way is needed — should have driver's license if possible.

▸ 1 Propmaster/Wardrobe — Pretty self-explanatory.

Whereas you'll need to get the four Superfriends to commit to all three days of the shoot, you can be a bit more flexible with the group listed above. You need to have all seven of these positions filled every day of filming, but this can be a changing cast. Continuity is a great thing; it saves time on the set not having to explain things more than once, but by the time you get to the bottom of this list, you may be running out of people willing to give up a whole holiday. Finding PAs willing to give you just a day might be easier.

So there is your crew. Including the slash, the whole crew is an even dozen. Forgive us but we have to say, a Dirty Dozen, ready to go to war (you get lots of war metaphors when you talk to filmmakers). With this group of twelve, you can tackle just about any problem. With this group, you can wind up with tremendous results.

HOW TO ASK A REALLY BIG FAVOR

Remember how we said at the beginning of the chapter that getting people to actually show up was one of the producer's big jobs? Good. Now listen carefully to the following suggestion.

Getting people to show up begins the moment you ask them to join the crew.

Do not ask people to be on your crew while passing in the halls. Don't ask on the cell phone. Don't send an e-mail. Don't IM. Don't be in a hurry, don't do it off-hand.

When you approach someone to be on the crew, ask if they have a minute. Find somewhere to sit down. As you ask if they'd be interested in being on the film crew, present them with a copy of the script. You should also attach a cover sheet, with their name and position, as it will appear in the credits, in large letters. Also include a job description.

We know this seems almost laughably formal. People you approach may at first be worried that something is wrong. This formality, however, serves an important purpose — it sets the tone. By making this formal approach, you communicate how serious this project is to you, and how important their role will be.

You've got to be serious if you want to pull off your shorts.

Allow us to rephrase.

The slash sets the tone. Set a serious tone from the outset, and people will take you seriously. If people take you seriously, they will show up, and maybe even be on time.

Once you have brought together your Dirty Dozen, it's time to collect those odd butterflies known as actors.

SCREEN TEST

You will want to have a formal and open audition for actors in order to cast your movie. Plaster your school with posters. Talk to the drama teacher and ask her to spread the word. If you have particular kids in mind for certain roles, go ahead and approach them and invite them to audition. The more kids you have to choose from, the stronger your cast will be. Do whatever it takes to attract a crowd. Pizza and soda may be called for here.

You will get a better turnout if you can manage to have auditions after school, somewhere on campus. You can also ask the drama teacher to use the theatre if your school has one, but just about any classroom will do. A room with a TV you can use as a monitor is a huge bonus.

You'll want to have the Associate Producer and Assistant Director with you at the audition. We would also strongly recommend that you turn your audition into a screen test. Ask the Camera Op and Sound guy to come and use all the equipment you have access to. Set up a monitor using available equipment or bring one from home (more about monitors in Chapter 8).

This will help you in a couple ways — first, it allows your crew to get some experience working together; second, it allows you to see how your actors are working on camera. You also can go back and look at the shot later, if you have any close calls or questions. And again, this footage may be useful to you as you are filling out a channel (although you will want to avoid posting anything that embarrasses your auditioners — consider cutting together only the successful auditions).

THE AUDITION

Before the audition, you'll have to decide which pieces of the script you want to hear from the actors. You'll want to pick one or two scenes from the script that feature the lead actors and some dialogue. You won't need long scenes. You'll be surprised how quickly you will be able to tell if someone is right or not. You may only need six lines of dialogue to get a feel.

In most cases, you can use one or two scenes with a couple of characters to cast everyone. Although it's preferable, you don't necessarily have to have actors read the parts you are considering them for. You can get a sense for the actors through having them read a part other than the one they may ultimately play. Having everyone read the same scene will keep the audition simple, and surprisingly, will still give you the information you need to fill all the roles, even the ones you don't have them read.

A note on audition material: you may write a script that has little or no dialogue. This is not unusual for a short film. And it's not an impossible problem for your audition. You don't have to have the actors read only from your script at the audition. What Hollywood movie is your film most like? Perhaps you can find that script and use a scene from that film as your audition material. It's perfectly okay to use a scene from another play or screenplay as audition material. Just make sure your actors know that they are performing material that will not be in your film. This avoids surprises later on.

THE AUDITION ROOM

For the audition, let the Assistant Director run the show. This will let her get used to her leadership role while the slash gets to focus on watching the actors. While the slash and the other crew members are in the audition room, the AD should be outside passing out scripts, deciding the order that actors go in, pairing actors and sending them in. It's a good idea to ask the actors to wait around after they have read once. You may want to see them read something else, or see a different pairing. The AD should also make clear where and when you will post a cast list.

It is very important that the AD make clear to every actor that is auditioning what the scheduled shooting dates are (you'll know more about scheduling in just a minute). You may even want to post the dates around the audition area. All the auditions are for nothing if your actor has to get wisdom teeth pulled during his big scene.

Inside the audition room, you are going to have to trust your gut and take careful notes.

Taking notes is going to be very important, particularly if lots of kids show up (and they might — being in a movie is cool). Make sure that you get every actor's name, and write down next to the name a distinguishing physical feature or clothing that will help you remember who was who.

(Consider bringing a digital still camera. Have the auditioners hold up a piece of paper with his or her name on it, then snap a photo.)

Consider coming up with a grading system, and ask your Associate Producer to use the same system (1-5 stars, 1-10, whatever works for you). Note which role they will play in the audition, and when they're done, where you could see them in the cast.

Follow the same routine with all the actors (again setting a professional tone). Don't fool around. Invite the actors into the room. Be nice; they're nervous. Ask for the personal information you need, check the camera, make your notes, and when you're finished say, "whenever you're ready." And away they'll go. As they do their stuff, you should be paying attention not to the actors, but to the monitor.

Watch kids with lots of stage experience very carefully. These kids may have lots of talent and experience, but may be used to hitting the back of the theatre with loud projecting voices and stagey gestures. These can knock the camera over. Stage acting and film acting are very different. Make sure stage actors can make the switch to the more subtle form by redirecting them.

A redirect is a suggestion offered by the director once the actors are finished with the audition piece — a request for a different take. It is one of the most useful aspects of an audition. They usually start with an "Okay, let try it again and this time..." Redirects are an expression of a director's personal style and vision, so make sure to think of redirects that work for you. You may want to have several canned redirects ready before you go into the audition.

Redirects are often suggestions of circumstances surrounding the scene. Some examples:

> "Okay, let's try it again and this time...."
> "Imagine you are talking to your best friend."
> "Imagine you just came from a friend's hospital room."
> "Imagine you are late for a test."

The redirects don't necessarily have to be appropriate to the scene. The direction you give may not be like the one you would give on the set.

You're just testing to see if the actor is flexible, can understand you, is willing to change, is easy to work with.

Most of all what you are looking for is an actor that can do the role with as little noticeable "acting" as possible.

CASTING

Once the audition is over, it's time to put kids in roles. Compare scores with your Associate Producer. Most of the decisions will be pretty clear. Trust your instincts. Go back to the tape if you need to.

If you have a tough one, the slash gets to make the final call.

Hopefully you had a ton of kids show up to the audition and you easily filled all the roles. But what if you don't really see the perfect person? What if the actor you really wanted didn't show up at the audition?

You may be tempted to go out and beg actors that you really want to be in your movie rather than cast the kids you weren't really crazy about at the audition. We think that you will be much better off casting kids that auditioned for one simple reason: they've already demonstrated that they will show up. Even those actors who aren't perfect, but show up at the audition are preferable to anyone you have to go and beg.

Actors that aren't perfect but show up are far better than excellent actors who don't.

The exception to this rule is if you just flat out don't get enough bodies to fill all the roles. In that case you might consider having a second audition. Lobby people to come out, ask what time works for them, and give the whole thing another shot.

If it is at all possible, require that your actors show up at some kind of audition. If an actor can't make an audition, they won't make the shoot.

Now that you have people, it's time for places.

LOCATIONS: SCOUT THEN SCHEDULE

Before you are able to create the shooting schedule (in the next chapter, you'll soon learn that the shooting schedule has nothing to do with the order things happen in the movie — it's all about practicalities), you'll need to pick the location for all of your shots. Each location will have its challenges, even though you will do your best to minimize these. You need to know *where* you are going to be before you know *what* you need and *when* you'll need it.

Obviously your script will be pretty specific about the kinds of places that you will need to shoot. Finding interesting locations contributes to a good-looking movie, but it's easy to go overboard when picking places to film. You will need to use your common sense and all your slash powers when picking locations. You'll have to balance art (writer/director) with practicality (producer). Always keep in mind that the coolest and most perfect locations may also pose the most challenges to filming. A perfect place doesn't guarantee a perfect shot if headaches overwhelm the film crew. You've got to look at location through the eyes of both the director and producer (how many eyes is that?).

Ask your AD and AP to come along for the ride to help you sort these things out.

WHEN PULLING OFF YOUR SHORTS, REMEMBER YOUR *PANTS*
Four things to scout for at any location:
> **P**ower
> **A**ccessibility
> **N**oise
> **T**raffic

Power — Remember that a film set is thirsty for electricity. Cameras, lights, monitors, sound equipment, all suck down power like a Hummer sucks gas. On your prospective location, where would be the closest outlet? Can you find power within the range of your extension cords (see equipment list)?

Accessibility — Where is your cast coming from? Where are they going to? It's good to keep in mind that this location may be only one of several shot during the day. If you're crossing state lines in search of a location, you may have gone too far. Try to keep locations clustered as much as possible. Keep travel time to a minimum for your cast and crew.

Noise — This can be a killer for a film crew. Make sure to get out of your car and listen carefully at your location. It's quirky when you think about it, but we tune out all kinds of ambient noise in real life, but we notice it when we're watching movies. Your audience will be distracted by traffic noise, air conditioners, power line hum, even excessive bird noise. Try to identify every sound you hear at your prospective location.

Traffic — Both the automotive and pedestrian kind can create a real headache for filmmakers. Heavily trafficked areas are hard to control. A fantastic location crawling with people (citizens, gawkers, starers, shot-fouler-uppers) may be less preferable than a less handsome spot with fewer onlookers.

Finding a place that you are familiar with and can control is a good thing. A house of a relative or close friend, school, a workplace of a relative are primo.

Finding locations to shoot that are close together will alleviate the scheduling crunch. So be creative about location. The camera can see as much or as little of a place as you want it to. Imagine all the possibilities your school, house, or neighborhood presents. Couldn't you shoot scenes at a doctor's office, a loading dock, a mad scientist's lab, a travel agency, a park — all on your campus? Can you find an adult who could help you get access? Imagine how much easier it is to schedule a day when you only have to move from one side of a building to another, rather than across town.

SHOOTING ON PRIVATE PROPERTY — THE FINE ART OF THE MOOCH

Remember that most places (aka locations) in this country are owned by somebody. And you had better get that somebody's permission before shooting. Don't be tempted, just because you don't see anyone around while you're scouting, to assume that nobody will mind if you make your movie in their field, neighborhood, store, empty lot, wherever. Always ask. Where possible, get permission in writing. A note on a scrap of paper is better than nothing.

Don't hop fences, don't assume it will be cool to use somebody's house, yard, or vacant lot, don't assume you can use a classroom, a field, wherever. Ask.

Nothing wrecks a tight schedule like getting tossed off a location in the middle of a shoot.

In general, you'll find that people will say yes if you ask nicely and in advance. You're a kid, after all, and people like kids. Do a little footwork. Ask around. Find out who owns the place and ask them using your best manners. This will pay off.

Your script can serve you well as a calling card. It's evidence of your seriousness. Give the owners a copy of your script and ask them to use their place. You'll have to promise to clean up after yourself which, of course, you will. It will be important that you give the owners very specific dates and times that you will need their place.

That's why the scheduling process described in the next chapter is so important.

PROPS/COSTUMES — FINDING CONTINUITY

We'll talk about budgeting more in chapters to follow, but your general philosophy should be: "I'm a kid. I have no money." Never spend money on anything if you can possibly help it. That should be applied first to the collection of props and costumes.

GIVING EVERYONE THEIR PROPS

Make a prop list by going back through your script and looking for every item that you will see in the shot. You'll want to create a master prop list, and also make note on the call sheets what props will be needed in a given segment. You'll want to think carefully, not just about the things that are mentioned explicitly in the script, but also the things that are implied.

If you have a scene in a classroom, don't think of just the book on the desk of your main character — what's on everyone else's desk? What's on the teacher's desk? What's on the walls? The more carefully you imagine these things, the better the movie will look.

Don't depend on finding any props at the location. You can't depend that the location will look exactly the way it did when you scout it. You want to control how your shot looks. Bring that look with you. Don't hope to discover something when you arrive.

Create prop lists for each of your six shooting sessions (see Chapter 5) on a separate piece of paper. Go by a liquor store and getting half a dozen wine case boxes. Paste one of your session prop lists on each one. Some props might have to move from box to box as you progress through the days, but this is a good way to keep things organized.

Do not buy props unless absolutely necessary. Think of the prop gathering process as a scavenger hunt. Borrow things, treat them well, and return them in good shape. Got a specific item in mind that you just can't find? Send out a mass e-mail to all your friends with the list of missing props. Let folks know their items will be immortalized in film. They may be more likely to share.

You may be very busy in the days leading up to the shoot, doing your director's preparation (see Chapter 6). This may be a good time to delegate to the Associate Producer. Give him the lists and boxes, and turn him loose.

RAGS

For the most part, the actors will provide their own costumes, but you need to give them each some guidance. There will obviously be a few pieces that you want to acquire — a T-shirt from a particular group, a tux, a specific kind of shoes, but for the most part, you can depend on the resourcefulness of your actors in this situation.

Create a list of characters, then sit down with your Assistant Director. Put down a few words next to each name that pertain specifically to costume. You don't have to be too specific, just some general idea. It should then preferably be the job of the AD to communicate with the actors. She should tell the actors to bring a couple things in a bag (not on them) to the rehearsal for you to choose from. More on that later.

ASK FIRST, SPEND LATER

If you absolutely can't find what you need anywhere but a store, don't go straight to the wallet. Whatever it is, small or large, see if you can get it donated first. Find a manager, fork over yet another script, explain the project and ask that the item be donated or loaned to the production. It's always worth a shot. In general, people want to help kids out. If they can't help, don't be a jerk. Take no as an answer and move on. The next time the answer might be yes.

THE REHEARSAL

The rehearsal is an important rally, not only to get the actors ready, but also to make sure the crew is ready to go for the shoot. The rehearsal would ideally be in an afternoon a day or two before the shoot, but practicality may require that you have it on the weekend before your shoot. The rehearsal shouldn't run longer than a couple hours.

The rehearsal is a chance for the actors to read through the script, but there are a number of other things to get done. You should absolutely require that everyone on the cast and crew be present.

There are a number of things you should accomplish at the rehearsal:

▶   Collect contact info – Try to get cell phone numbers for as many people in the cast and crew as possible. Encourage everyone to borrow or beg for a cell phone (this will really be helpful on the set). The Associate Producer should have all those numbers programmed into his phone.

▶   Costume check – Ask to see all the actors in costume, make choices about all the stuff actors have brought in. When the read-through begins, all the actors should be in costume – have your props/costumes person take notes about who is wearing what.

▶   Technical check – The full film crew should be in place to film the read through. They should be familiarizing themselves with equipment. The specific roles and tasks should be made clear.

▶   Introductions – The slash should let everyone know who everyone else is and what their role is.

▶ The Pitch — The slash should give the combined cast and crew a "pitch" which should include a synopsis of the movie, and a sense of what the movie means to the slash; a few words about style would be good.

▶ Read through — The actors should have the chance to read through the script at least three times. This is a chance to give a few notes to the actors — the slash should give the principal actors a few ideas about what he wants from them.

▶ Review the schedule (see Chapter 5) — Make sure everyone understands the call sheets and knows where you are going and when. (If you are shooting on a location unfamiliar to all — have maps available.)

When the rehearsal is over, have all the actors pull off their shorts, literally. Do not let actors take home their costumes! Ever! Missing costume pieces are a real headache for continuity (see Chapter 11), so don't let those actors leave wearing anything that will have to be in the film.

Now let's take a closer look at how all these people will come together — the schedule we referred to earlier — and talk about what all this is going to cost.

RESHOOT
Remember, the producer picks up the Oscar. Lay the groundwork for a successful shoot.

▶ Choose Superfriends very carefully, use adult input and personality profiles.
▶ Make a formal presentation when "hiring" crew members.
▶ Hold open, publicized auditions — make sure to redirect actors.
▶ Scout then schedule — remember your PANTS.
▶ Make thorough prop and costume lists — beg before you buy.
▶ Hold a rehearsal — all hands on deck.

CHAPTER **5**

TIME AND
MONEY

THE SCHEDULE AND THE (NON-EQUIPMENT) BUDGET

Sure, time is money, but what if you don't have much of either? It doesn't mean you can't make a great short film. It just requires that you be creative and resourceful — which just happens to be the qualities that make a good artist. Being short of time and money just demands that the slash be a better and more complete filmmaker.

You'll also have to show a little discipline and restraint. You'll need to create a strict schedule and budget and absolutely stick to them. Running over time is a particularly dangerous thing. If you don't create a clean and clear schedule and stand with it, your movie can easily get lost in the netherworld of the wannabe. If you do not stick with your schedule, and you go beyond the three-day shooting period we outline below, you will probably never finish your film. Your crew will disperse, other responsibilities will crop up, time will get tight, and the film will gather dust on your hard drive. Your shorts will not be pulled off.

Until this film is finished, you are not a filmmaker. Remember that getting it done is the one absolute rule of this process.

We know that creating and sticking to budgets and schedules is hard. If it were easy, everybody would be doing it.

TIMETABLE

Look at a calendar. It's time to find three days to shoot your movie. It is possible to find a day here, a day there. A few hours from time to time. It's possible to pull your shorts off a little at a time. But to keep together the cast and crew you need to make a professional film, to keep the momentum, we suggest that you find three continuous days on which to shoot your movie.

That means finding a holiday, and using it to make your film.

When choosing a holiday to shoot, we suggest that you go small — again.

Of course there are the biggies, the Daddies of the school year; Thanksgiving, Christmas, and Spring Break. These look, at first, like big sweeping open gaps in the school calendar — perfect for filming a short. Wrong. These long vacations are actually logistical nightmares, chock full of family conflicts, trips to Disneyland, nights at grandma's — a scheduling horror flick. Think you could get twenty-five people to find three days during Christmas to meet? Not a chance.

Pick on the little guys: three-day weekends such as Columbus Day, MLK, Presidents' Day, teacher work days. In general, people are less likely to have family obligations or be out of town on these holidays (though you'll still have some headaches getting everyone to stick around). Just one day off from school in combination with a weekend is enough to pull off those shorts.

SIX EASY PIECES

Time to cut your script into shreds. The task is to divide your script into six parts, each part containing scenes that have as much in common as possible, from a production point of view.

The six pieces come from three days of shooting, each with a morning (8:00 a.m. - 12:00 p.m.) and afternoon (1:00 p.m. - 5:00 p.m.) session. Let's refer to the sessions as Days 1, 2, and 3, and the sessions as M(orning) and A(fternoon).

The goal is to put about one page worth of material in each of the first five sessions, leaving the sixth session to pick up anything that you've missed.

Slug lines provide natural breaks in the script — dividing lines — scenes. Anytime several slugs have the same cast and location, this is called a sequence.

Group scenes and sequences that have roughly the same cast and location together until you have a page worth of material. (You may want to actually take scissors to a copy of the script.) You may be able to do slightly more than a page if you change location very little, or generally have a simple shot to get. If the shots are complex, try to do less than a page.

Once you have your five, one-page chunks, you need to pick one of your six time slots to put that page worth of scenes in.

Your actors might prefer if you tried to organize your day in the order that things happen in the script; unfortunately, the schedule usually doesn't allow for that. You may want to try to shoot roughly in order, but here are some other factors to consider.

▸ Place your more complicated sequences in morning slots. This gives you an opportunity to recover time in the afternoon if morning scenes run long and still stay on schedule. This also lets you attack tough scenes with a fresh cast and crew.

▸ Place your single most challenging sequence in 2M — by this time your crew will have gelled, the morning means you'll be fresh.

▸ If time gets tight, drop scenes or shots that don't require actors. You can pick these up in 3A. Landscapes, environmental shots, wide shots — you can go back and get these with a skeleton crew.

1M: 8:00 a.m. – noon Complex scenes
2M: 8:00 a.m. – noon Most Complex Scenes
3M: 8:00 a.m. – noon Complex Scenes

1A: 1:00 p.m. – 5:00 p.m. Simpler scenes
2A: 1:00 p.m. – 5:00 p.m. Simpler Scenes
3A: 1:00 p.m. – 5:00 p.m. Pickups, Background, Cast-less Leftovers

CALL SHEETS

Now that you have the general schedule laid out, it's time to fill out call sheets. Call sheets tell who has to show up where and when. They are the roll sheet for the cast and crew. Each shooting session will probably be subdivided into two or three call sheets. Call sheets cover a sequence or multiple sequences that have the same location and cast. The following is a suggestion for a simple and clear format for a call sheet.

DETENTION DEFICIT

Call Sheet

Tuesday 4/29/10

Call Time: 4 PM   Scene: Lab Rats
                                                  [come up with cute
                                                  titles]

Page: 3   Location: Chem Lab

CAST:
Character A: Joe Actor
Character B: Jane Actor

CREW:
Camera Op:
Gaffer:
Gaffer:
Sound:
Grip:
Wardrobe:
PA:
PA:

Notes:
[special props, costumes, special effects or production needs listed here]

You'll probably end up with a stack of 12-15 call sheets — bigger than your script by far. This will become your Associate Producer's bible. It's her job to keep you to the schedule. (You made it after all.) It's important that you stay absolutely committed to your schedule.

A note on call times: Dividing your four-hour M or A shooting segments into call sheets is going to involve some common sense estimates. Use the page as your guide, 1/4 page gets an hour. Dialogue takes slightly less time than action. Use common sense and you'll be fine.

MOOLAH

We'll say it again: Don't spend money, especially on production elements other than equipment (we'll talk more about equipment expenses in Chapter 8). You should be saving money for college, after all, just ask your parents. There is no reason that you shouldn't be able to scrounge 90% of the things you need on the set.

Park your pride. Repress all feelings of shame. Look cute and young and promising and like the hope of America for the future, then beg.

Now we're going to contradict ourselves. It will be impossible to spend no money on your film. There will be so many small things that they will almost inevitably add up to be real money. You need to be ready for that. Save in advance. Don't use credit cards. Pay cash.

You should also remember making a movie is not a bad investment. Having a film (or films or a "reel") to show to colleges and graduate programs further down the road can justify laying out some cash. Making a really tight professional film can get you positive attention from lots of different people (more in Chapter 12).

It's good to not spend money, but also good to remember that the money you are spending isn't just being thrown away.

FOOD/DRINK

The one place you will probably not be able to avoid spending a little money is on what movie types call "craft services," or food and drink to the rest of us.

There is a good reason to spend a little money in this area. A hungry film crew makes sucky movies. Keep them fed, even if it means spending a little money.

The essentials:

▶ Water, water everywhere — bottled is expensive; coolers full of ice water are cheaper — a must, particularly in warmer climates — there should be a source of water all the time on the set. Tell crew members to bring their own water bottles.

▶ Mix in sodas as you can afford it. Many a shoot has been fueled by Mountain Dew.

▸ Three lunches — enough to eat for the crowd. Work like crazy to avoid paying retail for more than one.

▸ A table full of snacks — Ask around, whatever junk they like best, set up where the munching wont screw up the sound. Mix in a bag of oranges, apples, bananas.

▸ Sunscreen — Keep a bottle on the craft services table and hope the PAs don't drink it. Very important if you are filming during sunny months — sunburn can mess with continuity!

The same beg and borrow idea you applied to props should follow you into the grocery store. Get to know the manager at your local food mart; find out if she's a film buff. Go to several until you find one that is. Whip that script out and share with her your challenge. You have twenty-five or so people, donating their time to your film, and you feel that it's up to you to keep them fed, caffeinated, and hydrated for three days. Do they have any dented cans or damaged packages that you could have?

If the grocery store manager doesn't come through, it's time to hit up the moms. Show the list of essentials to the moms of the Superfriends. See if they might be willing to take on a lunch, make contributions to the table.

If all else fails, there is always pizza. Though not the cheapest way to go, it's always a hit with the cast and crew. Lots of national pizza chains have a school rate. When you are placing your order, ask if they offer one, and take advantage of that.

At the end of the day, you are almost better off spending money on food than on props and costumes. If it comes down to one or the other, go for chow. Happy cast and crew make for happy films.

OTHER EXPENSES

Remember that cell phone minutes can add up, that cars burn gas, that if you break it, you pay for it.

THE BILL: WHAT'S THE DAMAGE?

An example of what out-of-pocket expenses you might anticipate in making your film (excluding equipment costs).

Video Rentals (Chapters 2 & 6)	8.00
Copies (scripts for reading, audition, cast and crew, handing out, set; posters; call sheets; shotboards, etc.)	35.00
Props	40.00
Costumes	35.00
Food (pizza for reading, 1 on-set lunch, snacks @ $10/session, sodas)	155.00
Contingency (you never knew money)	40.00
Total	313.00

The nice thing is that all these expenses won't be coming in at once. Obviously the reading comes weeks before the shoot. You can spread these expenses over several months. Still and all, over $300 is real money! This should demonstrate how quickly these expenses can add up and how important it is to get things for free whenever possible. Be careful with what you spend, be aggressive about asking for donations, and you can probably spend even less.

How low can you go?

When it comes to budget, go small. Sound familiar?

ASKING FOR MONEY

You want something that costs just over $300, but you're a kid and can't really put your hands on that kind of cash. What are you going to do?

Mom. Dad. Can we talk?

We're not at all opposed to hitting up the parents for a little cash. We feel like plowing $300 into an enduring work of art that could open doors for you later in life is a much better way to spend money than on an Xbox or a spree at Abercrombie.

Adults love to see teenagers hard at work at something. Being committed to something positive, something active — how can they not support your project? They will be particularly impressed when you hit them with the paperwork. Give them the whole deal: the script, the schedule, the call sheets, the shotboard (Chapter 6). Write out a budget (including equipment costs) and make a presentation. Even if your folks can't afford to give you a dime, you've impressed the heck out of them.

Be advised that if your parents decide to give you money, they're also going to feel free to give you some input — particularly if you have any controversial subject matter or language in your film. Listen patiently.

Even after all that, you may not get a nickel. Raising kids is expensive (we know you've never heard that before), and there is a fair chance that your folks won't be able to fork over cash. Be cool with that, show some understanding, and you may get help in other areas (making a lunch for the cast, for example).

Then it's time to move on to grandma.

Now you're just about set. The people, places and things are in place to make your movie. Everything is ready. Well, everything except for you. The director.

RESHOOT
Little time, less money, great movie. Being cheap and on time is an art form.

- ▸ Pick a long weekend to shoot the movie.
- ▸ Schedule in six blocks — three mornings, three afternoons.
- ▸ Create call sheets for cast and crew.
- ▸ Be a tightwad, but keep cast and crew fed and hydrated.
- ▸ Ask family for financial support, but take no for an answer.

6

DIRECTOR'S
PREPARATION

FONT TO FILM — A SHOTBOARD APPROACH

You've written the script and laid the groundwork for shooting your movie. The writer and producer badges of your slash have been earned. Now it's time to be a director.

Or rather to prepare to be a director. The task ahead of you is to take the tools that the producer (you) has given you, and use those to turn the script that the screenwriter (you) has given you into an effective film. Time to take words on a page and transform them into visuals. This transformation will require that you start thinking in a new way. You'll have to think with your eyes.

To accomplish this little act of alchemy, professional directors put in countless hours in preparation before they ever set foot on a set. This preparation varies from director to director, but it usually involves a couple of things: drafting storyboards and writing up a shot list.

On a Hollywood movie, the storyboards end up looking like something from the pages of a comic book or graphic novel. Every individual shot is sketched almost exactly as it will appear on the screen (usually by a professional artist hired by the producer to work with the director). Each frame of the storyboards contains information about movement of characters and camera. They tell a clear visual story.

The script is also converted into an incredibly detailed document, the shot list. This list describes every second that the camera rolls — every angle and reverse angle, wide shots to close-ups. All will find their way onto the shot list.

Like you've got time for all that.

Because you are a student and presumably have obligations other than just preparing to make your movie (remember homework?), we suggest a process of preparation that is not as time consuming as what the pros do. Consider combining storyboard and shot list into a single document — a shotboard (storylist?).

Though your time is precious, we do believe that time spent preparing is clearly worth it. Every minute you spend getting ready to film is a minute you will save on the set. It's a tiny step toward making your movie better.

The purpose of the preparation is to be thoughtful and imagine how you will translate words into pictures.

WATCH AND LEARN

Start by going back into the dark. It's time to watch movies again. We hope you held on to the movie and screenplay that you put together back in the writing chapter because you'll want to look at them again from another perspective. You'll also want to pick up a new flick or two.

Think about what movies you can name that you would like your movie to be like. Think of two or three. Of course your movie will be utterly original and expressive of your very personal style, but you might need to do a little stealing as well.

So maybe there isn't a movie out there that is exactly like your movie, but there is probably one that is at least related — get that one. Can't think of a movie? Find a word from the following list that you think best describes your movie and choose from our list of recommendations. If you are younger than 17, check with your parents about getting an R-rated movie.

Goofy
Raising Arizona
American Pie

Creepy/Atmospheric
Alien
28 Days Later

Intense
Ronin
Traffic

Witty/Satirical
Wag the Dog
The Royal Tenenbaums

Intricate
The Shawshank Redemption
The Usual Suspects

Once you've picked your model movies, head to the local video store (they probably know you by name now) or revisit your Netflix cue. Try to find your movie on widescreen format DVD if possible, but any format will do.

THREE EXERCISES
Exercise A) Script to Screen
Watch the movie with the screenplay in your lap again. Last time, you were keeping your eye on the script, with the idea that you were learning how screenwriters express themselves on the page. This time, you'll be looking for how directors translate those words onto the screen. Roll the movie, this time keeping your attention mostly on the screen. Check in on the script frequently.

Notice how the director translates a stage direction into a series of shots. Observe how exchanges of dialogue are filmed from multiple angles and distances.

How does the filmmaker stitch together the story? How does this filmmaker turn words into pictures?

Exercise B) Establishing Style — Reverse Storyboarding
Load one of the movies that you want your movie to be like. This time when you sit down to watch, you will want a notebook and the remote for the DVD player. The objective of this exercise is to develop a sense of visual style. How do these directors create a mood or feel for their films through choices they make in how to shoot a scene?

Roll the movie. As soon as things get interesting, when something looks cool or distinctive or you just get the impulse, hit the pause button on the remote.

Pause 1

Note color, light, and shadow. What kind of picture is the director painting? What colors appear? Bright and saturated or muted and earthy? What is the quality of the light? Are there shadows? How does the director use these elements to create a feeling, an emotional tone for the movie? Write it down.

Roll again.

Pause 2

This time note how all the elements are arranged within the frame of the movie. Where are the characters placed in relation to the objects around them? Is the shot wide — encompassing lots of the environment; medium — taking in mostly people; a close shot? Where is the camera placed: close to the ground, eye level, above the action? How does the composition of the shot change the way the viewer feels about the action on the screen?

Roll the movie.

Pause 3

Using the top half of a page, sketch what you see on the screen. Artistic perfection is not called for here. Try to suggest all the major elements, buildings, cars, trees, people. It's okay if the result reminds you of third-grade Mother's Day cards. Stick figures are perfectly fine. If you want to suggest motion, throw some arrows in there.

Congratulations, you've just storyboarded a shot for the first time. Only you just did it in reverse.

Try the exercise with a couple of the movies you want yours to be like.

Exercise C) Covering Coverage

Load the screenplay/movie again.

The purpose of this exercise is to familiarize you with the process of creating a scene using multiple shots, to give you a feel of all the different angles and perspectives you may want for any given moment in the movie. The collection of shots you get for any given scene is referred to as "coverage." Having enough coverage is going to be very important to the editor (you) later in the process.

Go to your published screenplay and pick a slug line and the scene that follows, preferably one that has a little bit of dialogue, preferably one that is on the short side. We're just going for one slug to the next slug here. Find that scene in the DVD of the movie.

Roll the movie, but hit pause every time that the movie cuts from one shot or camera angle to another. You'll need a quick thumb here. It may take a couple passes through to get them all. Make a brief note about what is in the shot (close, wide, who's in the shot, etc.) Keep this up until you reach the next slug line.

Congratulations, you've made a shot list. Only in reverse.

How many different shots are on your list? Surprised? Compare that to what you find in the script. You get a feeling for how many ways the director shoots every scene, and how the editor creates a tapestry from that coverage into the movie you see on screen. Keep this coverage in mind as you make notes in preparation for the shoot.

CREATING THE SHOTBOARD

Your shotboards should be relatively simple to create — a good way for you to clarify your thinking before you get on the set, and also a nice communications tool for use with your crew. You are going to combine the (reversed) exercises above. Draw a line through a piece of standard notebook paper: above the line goes a sketch (storyboard), and below the line go your notes (shot list). You can also draw the line vertically — pictures to the right and words to the left, or vice versa.

In order to keep the time commitment reasonable, don't create more than one shotboard per slug line. You should probably have no more than four shotboards per morning or afternoon shooting session, or a total of 20-25 for the whole project.

When looking at a scene or sequence, choose the widest or most visually complex shot in the sequence to put above the line. Again, the artistry here need not warrant framing. You don't have to be Michelangelo. Stick figures are fine. At least you will be thinking about composition before you get on the set. You'll have something to show the crew when explaining what you're going for. This process will be much easier if you have scouted your locations already. You can sketch what you know (or hope) will be there.

Below the line take some notes about other shots and angles. Describe in a few words and phrases what you want to see in this sequence. This section could end up looking a lot like exercise C above. A laundry list of shots you need for each sequence. You don't need complete sentences. Bullets will do just fine. Make some notes about coverage that you may want if you have enough time.

When making notes, be sure to prioritize your shots. Work top to bottom, from the shot you absolutely must have, to shots you need to tell the story, to coverage that would probably be useful in editing, to nifty little pickups that are cool but not essential. This priority list will help you if time starts to get tight. Know what you can drop before you are faced with that difficult decision on the set.

Remember that you have scheduled your most complicated material for your morning sessions. If your preparation time is limited, give these sessions the bulk of your shotboards.

Once your shotboards are complete, make copies for all of the Superfriends. Schedule a meeting with all of you where you sit down with these and the script and you walk them through the whole set, pointing out what you feel to be the most important visual features of each moment.

Take your Assistant Director aside. Tell her to guard her shotboards well. They will guide her through the wilderness of the shoot. She should never stray from them. They should never be out of her possession from the time you present them to her until you wrap the shoot. She should consider laminating and sleeping with them (kidding... sort of).

Now that you have completed your director's preparation, it's time for the real deal. It's time to shoot your movie.

RESHOOT
Director's prep: Thinking with your eyes.

- ▶ Combine storyboards and shot lists into "shotboards."
- ▶ Practice by creating shotboards in reverse, using movies you love.
- ▶ Share the shotboard with your Superfriends — walk them through the movie.

AS IF THE CAM WERE A CHARACTER ITSELF

ONIMOUS: fog? shadow?

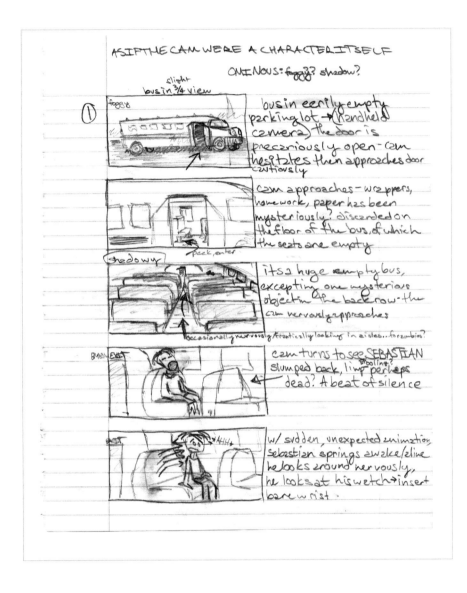

① bus in eerily empty parking lot → (handheld camera) the door is precariously open - cam hesitates then approaches door cautiously

cam approaches - wrappers, homework, paper has been mysteriously? discarded on the floor of the bus, of which the seats are empty

its a huge empty bus, excepting one mysterious object in the back row - the cam nervously approaches

cam turns to see SEBASTIAN slumped back, limp - perhaps dead? A beat of silence

w/ sudden, unexpected animation, sebastian springs awake/alive he looks around nervously, he looks at his watch → insert bare wrist.

CHAPTER

7
RINGMASTER
THE EYE ON THE MONITOR

IT'S ALL ABOUT YOU

The big moment is here. Time to roll. Get ready for an amazing experience. It's time to be a director on a film set. Giddyup.

The thing about being a director on a movie set, it's fun and all, but everything in that universe depends on you. No pressure. You are the leader of the film set, and the set will be a reflection of you. If you are prepared, confident, even-tempered and good-humored, your crew (and your movie) will be, too. If you are frazzled, grumpy, and disorganized... You get it.

THE DIRECTOR ON THE SET

You have three primary jobs on the set: coordinating, communicating, and decision-making. Coordination of the elements of camera, sound, and performance is one of your main responsibilities. You are the mix-master, making sure that all the many elements are in the proper blend. You must constantly be aware of how these pieces are coming together as a whole, making sure that all are working together in concert.

Communicating what you are looking for to the cast and crew is an essential part of your duties. As the director, you will talk as much or more than you will do. You will need to communicate with every single person on the set. In this communication you need to be clear and concise, without being bossy or demanding or condescending. In communication with actors, camera operators, grips, or anyone else, you will need to get to the point, while always, always, always remaining respectful.

Decisions, decisions, decisions. Do you want the camera here or here? You want the book in or out of the frame? Do you have money for more sodas? Do you like these shoes? How tall should the flames be? Making decisions is your primary job. You will get offered options and asked questions, sometimes several at once. It's okay to be thoughtful, but on the set you are not going to have the time to linger over decisions. Follow your instincts. Going with your first thought is probably the way to go. Efficiency is more important than perfection.

Sometimes you are going to be asked so many questions that it will drive you a little nuts. Tough. Answering questions is your job so get over yourself, make a decision, be nice, and move on toward pulling off your movie.

It is essential that you remain calm and respectful throughout the shoot. This is particularly important as things get difficult. You must remain calm. If you let the temperature rise, people are going to walk. If the set gets unpleasant, your crew will evaporate. After all, what's keeping them there? If the environment is harsh and tension-filled, why stick around? The big payday? Yeah, right.

You the man, you got the power, it's your show — now be nice.

THE AP AND AD

Make sure the Associate Producer and Assistant Director know their responsibilities on the set.

Associate Producer

▸ Takes roll at the beginning of each session. Makes sure everyone remembers their job, has a script in his pocket. Calls those that are missing.
▸ Monitors slush pile of scripts.
▸ Keeps an eye on the food table. Makes sure food and drinks are kept away from filming area — spills can wreck the tech. Help from PAs in this area.
▸ Troubleshooting missing, broken production elements, problems of any kind.
▸ Keeps the director on schedule — the woman with the watch.
▸ Advance team to next location as set wraps.

The AP is the person that smoothes the road for the production, diffuses problems as they arise, keeps everyone fed and hydrated, and keeps everything moving along. The AP should be popular with everyone on the set, with the exception of the director. The AP should be a bug in the director's ear whenever time gets tight.

Assistant Director

▸ Makes sure the crew knows exactly what the director wants.
▸ Directs crew to the next setup or shot.
▸ Keeps crew focused and on-task.
▸ Assists crew in a pinch with whatever needs doing.
▸ Available for advice to director on creative decisions.
▸ Monitors script and shotboard to make sure coverage is complete.

The AD is the straw boss, the sergeant of the set — a nice sergeant. This person makes clear what the next move is for each and every crew member on the set. The voice that the crew will hear most often will be the AD's, not the director's. The AD should spend most of the production right at the director's shoulder, giving an opinion when asked, waiting to hear what has to happen, and making it work. The AD is also crossing off scenes and shots from the script, making sure that nothing is left out (a crucial duty).

THE HUDDLE

Start each session, morning or afternoon, by pulling the cast and crew together and setting out your objectives for that session. This will get everyone focused and moving in the same direction. Remind everyone to turn their cell phones off.

Then it's time to roll; the camera and sound should be setting up, gaffers hanging lights where necessary, actors getting into costume, director watching the monitor and framing the shot. If you are on a location that has traffic, the AD should be strategically placing PAs with phones or walkie-talkies to hold people/cars back when the cameras are rolling.

Then comes the time when everyone is in place and ready. Time to get your first shot.

ACTION!

You actually get to say that, and say it loud. And several other things, too. Though it may seem cheesy, there is a reason you yell a specific series of orders when shooting on the set, and it goes back to communication. It's important for everyone on the set to know what is up, so nobody botches the shot.

Here is the traditional sequence of verbal orders used by the director and the crew during the shoot. Lots of people have to act on these signals, so be loud and clear.

SHOOTING SHOUTING

1) "Lock it up!" — Assistant Director (AD) — tells PAs to hold all traffic, camera is about to roll. Everyone should take this as the signal to be quiet. (If people don't get it, the AD can shout "Quiet!") Note that the AD is doing most of the shouting, thereby letting the director concentrate.

2) "Sound?" — AD — asks the sound crew if they are ready.

3) "Speed!" — Sound Op — signals that the sound equipment is working and that he is ready from this moment forward to get good sound.

4) "Camera?" — AD — asks the camera operator if he is ready. By this point the PA has put the slate (the clicker) inside the frame so that the camera person can see it.

5) "Rolling!" — Camera Op — signals that the camera is working, he can see the slate, and he has pressed record. We're filming!

6) "Scene 5, Take 2" — PA — still holding the slate in front of the camera. The scene number comes from the script you wrote. This helps to organize your footage later. No need to click the slate unless you have multiple cameras, but it might be fun to do so.

7) "Action!" — Director — signals the actors that it's time to do their stuff.

8) "Cut!" — Director — signals everyone that the shot is finished. This allows the camera operator to press the red button and stop recording.

9) "Back to one!" — AD — signals everyone to go back to their positions at the beginning of the shot. We're going again. Time for another take.

10) "Moving on!" — AD — signals that the director got the shot and it's time to move on to the next one. The AD will then announce what the next shot is.

11) "That's a location wrap!" — AD — signals everybody that it's time to move on to the next location.

12) "That's a wrap!" — AD — lets everyone know that's it for the day.

It's important that these signals only be given by the people listed above. If anyone other than the director yells "cut," real confusion and problems can arise. Everyone should stick to their lines, and make the routine consistent. Once the crew gets used to the routine, the probability of a mistake drops if you do it the same way every time.

HOW YOU KNOW YOU'VE GOT IT

Some times it will be crystal clear when you get the shot that you want. Everything clicks. It's like the image in your head has been grafted onto the monitor as if by telepathy. Magic. Have a couple of these during the course of the day and you should write home to mom.

More often, you shoot until you get as close as you can to what you want before time runs out. Typically, with your input to the technical folks and actors, each take will get closer and closer to what you want until you feel ready to move on. Your last take will be your best. Getting the shot is a balance of artistic concerns (wanting what's in your head), and practical ones (time). Be patient, communicate between takes about what you want, what you want changed, then roll again. Don't expect that just because you're doing another take, that the shot will get better — you have to make clear what you want. You have to talk!

If you have the luxury, you will always want to get multiple takes of almost any shot. You will be grateful for this during editing. It gives you more choices, and choices make better-looking films.

Get as much coverage as you can. Shoot from multiple distances and angles, but when the AP tells you that time is running short, you simply must respect that. Maybe you have time for one more take if you feel you are nearing perfection, but overall you have to respect the AP. It's good to worry about getting the shot, but the schedule is about the whole movie. Having a perfect shot doesn't matter unless you get the whole film in the can. The schedule should beat the shot every time.

GETTING THE PERFORMANCE — COACHING ACTORS
Much of the work that you do on the set will concern getting the performance that you want from your actors. In all your dealings with actors it is very important to remember that acting is a risky business. These guys are hanging it all out there for everyone to see (talk about pulling off your shorts).

Seriously, you are asking your actors to make themselves vulnerable. They're going to get their faces splashed all over a movie screen for all to laugh at. Being vulnerable like that is particularly hard on two kinds of people: inexperienced actors and teenagers. You have people in your cast that are both.

So be patient, make sure that your cast feels safe. Never laugh or mock what they are doing. Offer lots of positive encouragement.

GO SMALL YET AGAIN
You are probably going to have to work with your actors to "go small" with their performance.

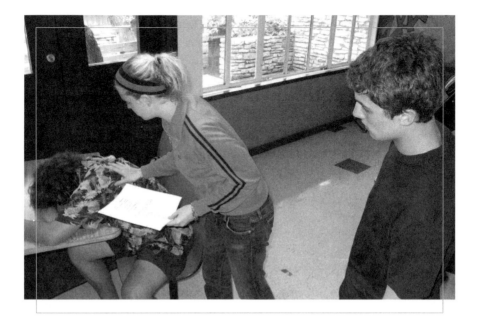

If your actors have any experience at all, it's probably on the stage, which may actually work against them. Because stage actors are trained to "project" — to reach the back of the auditorium with voice and gestures, their work for the camera may seem exaggerated. Even actors with no experience probably have an idea of acting that calls for "putting on a character" — doing things other than what comes naturally.

In general, you want to encourage your actors to "act" as little as possible, to be natural. (This will not always be true. If you are working in a non-realistic, or stylized mode, you may be looking for something else.) In order for actors to be natural, to be more honest on tape, you need to get them to relax.

It may sound silly, but you may need to remind your actors to breathe. Breathing deeply is an important part of relaxing, and relaxing is an important part of seeming natural on film. If an actor seems stiff or tense, ask them to jump around for a minute, to shake it out, and to breathe. This helps them to relax. Tell them not to act. That they're doing great.

DON'T DO IT LIKE I DO

In giving the actor guidance, avoid the temptation to act it for them yourself as you want it. This practice, known as "giving a line reading" will not ultimately get the result you want. A line reading puts the actor in the position of just imitating you. If the actor is not a good mimic this will lead to an awkward performance. The actor needs to find the performance for herself for it to look honest on film. Instead, give them analogies or metaphors; draw parallels to real life that they might have experienced. "It's just like when you...."

You may also want to ask questions of the actor, to help the actor discover things about the character he or she is playing. Asking actors about the motivation of their character can often lead to a breakthrough. Ask the actor what he or she wants in a scene, what they are after from the people around them. What is their objective?

SQUASH THE IMPROV BUG

We've all heard stories about actors making up lines on the set, improvising whole scenes that were just amazing and brilliant. We strongly suggest that you discourage actors from changing their lines. You may even want to assign the AD to keep an eye on the script and correct actors if they stray from what's written.

Once an actor starts improvising, she'll never stop. In some cases the improv might be better than what you've written, but most of the time it won't be. Maybe one actor is gifted in improv, but others stink on ice. How do you manage that? Everything will run more smoothly, and you'll end up with a more professional product if all your actors just stick to the script.

Overall, working with actors is a ball. The best thing about actors is that they make you look great. All their creativity and talent is contributed toward making your vision come true. They'll add dimensions that you never imagined. They'll take your world and add to it and make it better. Actors are amazing. Be grateful for them.

MOVING VIOLATIONS

You've finally gotten the perfect take, and you are finished at a location. It's time to move. Almost.

CHECK THE GATE

Before you budge, before anyone unplugs a cord, before an actor can escape, before anyone touches a light, it's time to "check the gate." This is another one of those nifty movie-guy phrases that means "make sure that you got it." Before you tear down your set, have the camera op rewind the tape and check to make sure that the footage is actually in the camera. Once you get the set down, you'll never be able to get it back up again just as it was. Therefore if you want to avoid a continuity nightmare (more on that later) you need to make sure you have the footage you need before moving on.

Once you have checked the gate, the real danger begins.

COLLATERAL DAMAGE

Standing outside a house as the guys with the dollies hoisted the sofa onto the moving truck, a wise man was heard to say "three moves equals a fire." Which is another way of saying, motion is destruction. The same idea applies to your movie set.

Every time you move the set, every person and piece of equipment is at risk. This may make us sound like old men (we are), but you must be very cautious and deliberate when you move. You are about to put a lot of expensive electronic equipment in the air. Even when time is tight (especially when time is tight), you and the AD need to encourage everyone to take their time. The time you save by rushing will be very expensive in terms of busted stuff.

You are the slash, so you set the example. Don't rush. Since the monitor is your friend, assign yourself as the monitor grip. Be careful as you pack and transport the monitor. Others will follow your lead.

PERSONAL DAMAGE

Take care of yourself.

The three days of the shoot are incredibly intense for the slash. All your time and hard work comes down to this short period of time. You have to hold the whole enterprise together, make a million decisions, work long hours, and generally stress out.

One thing that you should feel confident about: If you have followed the suggestions of this book, you are extremely well prepared. That should give you some confidence, and allow you to relax a bit. You are ready for this. Because you are prepared, there is no reason to stay up late cramming or stressing. Get plenty of sleep during the shoot — eight hours a night minimum.

Also make sure that during the excitement of the shoot you don't forget to eat right and drink plenty of water. A well-hydrated brain works better (an actual scientific fact!). There may be times that you can't leave the monitor, but if you are polite, you can probably ask the AD to bring you something to eat or drink. Don't get so wrapped up in what you are doing that you forget to take care of yourself.

WORST-CASE SCENARIOS

We hesitate to even write this section.

What follows are obstacles that we hope you never have to face. The big hassles that can really impact your movie. In general, we think you need to keep the production you have set in motion rolling forward, even if it's a compromise. It is very hard to get everyone and everything together and on the set. Don't give up. Adapt and move ahead in whatever way you can manage.

We could just avoid the subject and hope for the best, but we think you should know. Brace yourself.

No Shows

It's time to shoot the big climactic scene, and your star is nowhere to be found. She's not answering her cell phone. Her parents aren't home.

Twenty-five people are standing around. The clock ticks slowly. Disaster. Give it ten minutes, then recast. This is relatively simple if this is the missing actor's first scene, more nightmarish if that is not the case.

If possible, move an actor in a small role into a bigger one. If that won't work, use absolutely anyone on the set that you think will work and will agree to do it. Avoid doing it yourself if at all possible. This casting change may mean that you have to go back and re-shoot some scenes. Do your best. This is the kind of thing your last afternoon (3A) is for.

Stormy Weather

You're scheduled to shoot in the park. It's pouring.

Do a dance. Say a prayer. Juggle the schedule.

Got anything you can shoot inside? Can you adapt the screenplay to work inside? You are better off adapting and moving forward than giving up the day. The schedule is meant to be an optimal arrangement, but you'll have to respond to what you're given.

Bad weather is a headache to all filmmakers no matter what the level, no matter what the budget. If the weather messes with your movie, you can at least take comfort in the fact that you are in good company. It's happened to everyone.

Glitch

It's such an innocent little word. But one of these in your camera can bring the whole set to a halt. Be careful with the equipment, and this is an unlikely circumstance. However, tech is tech, and bugs can happen.

Give it ten minutes, then find another camera. Doesn't matter what kind. Find something that rolls. The people that you have gathered together are far more important that the quality of the video equipment and image, so find something.

You may even consider having this backup on the set. Mom got a camcorder? Bring it along even if it does not match your other camera. Get it in the can, and fix it in post. "Fix it in post" means to correct problems when you are editing.

THAT'S A WRAP

Nothing feels better to a filmmaker than those three words. The sense of relief and satisfaction that will run through you will be overwhelming. You prepared, you rolled with the punches, and you got it in the can.

Congratulations.

But you haven't pulled off your shorts quite yet. Time for "post."

RESHOOT

Rolling: Sitting in the director's chair.

- ▶ Be ready to communicate, coordinate, and make decisions.
- ▶ Make sure the AD and AP know their jobs, huddle with everyone before you roll.
- ▶ Using the same set of calls before letting cameras roll limits confusion.
- ▶ Be patient and supportive of vulnerable actors.
- ▶ "Check the gate" before moving calmly and slowly to the next location.
- ▶ Take care of yourself on the set, beware of fatigue and dehydration.

CHAPTER **8**

EQUIPMENT

So you've got your hands on a video camera and now you are making a movie. Remember, there are a bunch of other people out there who claim to be doing the same thing you are. And the main reason that they think they can make a movie is because they own a camera. Plain and simple: Camera = Movie.

If all you use is a video camera in your production then it's going to look (and sound) like home video, plain and simple. But if you can get your hands on just five more pieces of equipment, then you will immediately take yourself out of the beginner category. These five items are a tripod, a shotgun microphone, a reflector, a television monitor, and black plastic.

We have to be really careful in this chapter not to scare you with a bunch of gear recommendations. Don't think that you have to buy, rent, or borrow everything you see here. You don't. But if you want your movie to look and sound good, work really hard to get the five pieces we just mentioned.

The rest of this chapter explains these five pieces as well as a whole mess of equipment that you could use. Again, don't feel like you have to buy all of it. Try to borrow some equipment from your drama department or make some of the pieces yourself. As you sift through it all, pay close attention to lights, the dolly, the camera stabilizer, the wide-angle lens, and the jib arm. These extra five pieces of equipment will catapult you out of the beginner category.

At the end of this chapter you will find two gear lists: one for a low-budget teen production and the other for a high-budget teen production.

THE CAMERA

You may already have a camera, but read this section anyway since you might want to upgrade for your big production.

If your parents offered you the choice of either a car or a video camera for your birthday, which would you choose? The car buys you freedom. You and your friends get to go where you want and when you want. No more quietly calling mom from the multiplex to let her know the movie is over and you need a ride home.

Or, you could choose the camera. You get to make your own movie and invite all your friends to the premiere. It gets you a scholarship to film school. You make a million bucks, and you buy your parents a car for their birthday.

On a more realistic note, maybe that special person in history class will finally notice you. Every other schmo has a car, but you are a filmmaker. This makes saying hello a lot easier: "Hey, I am making this film; do you want to help out?" There is no commitment, and yet who knows where it might lead.

So, if the opportunity exists to get your own camera, by all means do so — not only for dating purposes, but also because you are serious about becoming a filmmaker. Right? You need your own camera to practice your craft. Plus you will get to make movies all the time.

WHAT KIND OF CAMERA TO GET

Regardless of how you get a camera, get the highest quality video camera you can. While award-winning shorts have been sewn with low quality cameras, nicer cameras tend to make prettier pictures because of their better lenses, larger image sensors, higher number of image sensors, and better overall electronics. The nicer the camera, the more you can concentrate on the rest of the production.

HVX200

When looking for a camera, one buzzword will take you a long way: "three-chip camera." Okay, okay, it is more than one word. Get over it. Another buzzword that might be helpful: "prosumer" (which means professional and consumer and is two words posing as one).

Here are some more detailed suggestions of what to look for. They are just suggestions — make a movie no matter what camera you have.

▶ **Film vs. Not Film:** When you go to film school you will do some work on film, but make this short on some other medium. It might be digital tape, or cards, or discs, all of which are way cheaper than film. Film also requires a lot more experience to make it look good.

▶ **High Definition:** If you have your hands on an older camera, it might be a Standard Definition, or SD, camera. This means that the picture has 720 vertical and 480 horizontal lines of resolution in North American countries (called NTSC) or 720 x 540 in Europe and beyond (called PAL). High Definition means more lines of resolution, which usually makes for a sharper picture. There are two common flavors of HD: 1280 vertical by 720 horizontal lines of resolution and 1920 vertical by 1080 horizontal lines of resolution. So, HD means a better image, usually. Be careful though since a cheap HD camera can look bad. All HD really means is resolution. It tells you little about the quality of the lens or the depth of the color being captured. HD can look awful, and there are SD cameras that are far better than HD cameras.

▶ **Three-Chip Cameras:** Your kindergarten teacher lied to you. Not knowing that you would be a filmmaker some day, he or she listed the primary colors as red, blue, and yellow. This works if you are mixing paints. But what if you are mixing light? You are now a filmmaker who paints with light, and the primary colors for light are red, green, and blue. A three-chip camera divides light into these primary colors, and as its name implies, it has a receiver (chip) for each color. If a camera has only one chip, then that one chip does all the work, and it has to make some compromises. If you get a three-chip camera, you are almost guaranteed to have everything else on our list since three chip cameras are high-end to start with. Chips may also be called CCDs. They vary in size, and bigger is better. If you cannot get a three-chip camera, then don't worry. Make your film anyway.

▶ **Audio In:** Read this paragraph as many times as it takes to memorize it. It is more important than anything we write in this chapter. Make sure that you can use an external microphone with your camera. Using the microphone that is on your camera will often result in hollow and far-away-sounding audio. An external mic is the number one tool in making movie magic. On some cameras, the mic in is similar to the plug on your headphones. On higher end cameras it is a three-pronged XLR plug.

▶ **LCD Screen:** Some cameras have a flip out screen which shows you what is being recorded. These are a really nice feature, but not a must have. They are hard to see in strong sunlight. They are no substitute for the monitor we list later in this chapter.

▸ **Manual Focus:** You must have complete control of your focus. If not, then you are forced to use autofocus, which has this nasty habit of focusing on the tree in the background rather than your main actor in the foreground. Even worse, it will go back and forth between the two. It makes for an ugly picture that is guaranteed to put you into the beginner category. There is no compromise here.

▸ **White Balance:** White light from the sun is different than white light from a light bulb. Some cameras have a setting that allows you to set the camera for shooting in sunlight or under a light bulb. Even better are the cameras that allow you to adjust the white balance setting for any sort of light. This feature is usually called Manual White Balance.

▸ **Image Stabilization:** Most cameras will have this feature. And while you should usually avoid any sort of electronic manipulation of your image, image stabilization is your friend.

▸ **Progressive Scan:** This helps video to look like film by enabling the camera to take one picture at a time, just like film. The opposite of Progressive Scan Video is Interlaced Video. Interlaced video combines the present frame and the previous frame to make for a smoother and cleaner picture. But it looks too clean, and looks more like a soap opera on TV than a film on the big screen. There are ways to fix interlaced video using a computer program, so don't worry too much about this one.

▸ **Name Brands:** We like Canon, Sony, Panasonic, and JVC. Other brands make good cameras too, so shop around.

HOW TO BUY A CAMERA

Big, near-the-mall electronics stores might carry some three-chip cameras, but your best local bet will be an actual photography store. If you have a particular brand that you like, then you can go to that brand's website and find dealers near you. Or you can shop on the net, which usually proves cheaper than local purchases. Be careful though, as there is a shady side to Internet electronic sales. Be sure to ask if the camera is new, in a box, and factory sealed. Also check on the company's return policy. Mom or Dad can help you with this. Big online stores include B&H photography (which also sells used equipment) and J&R photography as well as Best Buy.

Buying used equipment can be a little iffy, so you may want to get an adult to help out. Find someone — anyone — in your life that knows a little bit about cameras and ask for a second opinion before you buy. There are two advantages to buying used equipment. First, it is a lot cheaper. Second, you sometimes find people selling all their gear at once, so you might also get a tripod. The biggest drawback is that the camera may be damaged.

A last note about buying. If you already have a camera, then you and your parents may be a little hesitant to shell out even more dough. In that case, think about renting or borrowing a three chip for the big shoot.

In the end, use what you have, even if it is a one-chip camera.

HOW TO BORROW A CAMERA

First and foremost, when you borrow a camera be sure to get it long enough so that you can actually use it before your shoot. Take some shots and then look at them on a television. You will also need the camera after the shoot to load the video onto a computer.

> Once you have bought the camera, ask your parents to put it on their insurance policy. They will think you are growing up to be an upstanding and financially responsible human being.

If you borrow a camera, remember that you are asking someone to use his or her very expensive piece of equipment. Look responsible and show him or her your game plan. Your chances of getting to borrow the camera are greater if the owner thinks you have your ducks in a row and are really going to go through with your plan. Tuck in your shirt and take out your eyebrow stud. Most important of all, print out a copy of your script and be prepared to give him or her one. Your script says: "I really am making a movie."

Your friends and family are the best bet for borrowing a camera. Work it. Ask mom and dad if they have one at their jobs. Find the uncle who runs a wedding video business or that cousin who gets an employee discount at Best Buy.

If you're a student, look to your own high school, and look beyond the drama department. Foreign language departments are notorious for asking their students to make petit skits on camera. Science teachers are filming projectile motion all the time. Football teams love to watch their games over and over again, so see if the athletic department has a camera. And if your high school doesn't pan out, look to friends at other high schools.

Explore contacts at colleges and universities. Most every academic department at a university has some sort of access to a video camera. Some universities offer after-hours courses for the community in everything from waltzing to scuba diving to video production. Finally, even if you are in high school, think about taking an actual course at the local community college. You will get access to a lot of equipment.

Look to your local cable access channel. Such channels often have programs in which they train you to use their equipment, which might not be a bad thing. The catch is that you have to show your work on their channel, which is definitely not a bad thing!

Look to other organizations. Some towns have clubs dedicated to youth cinema. Maybe they have cameras. Churches use video cameras a lot. The Boy Scouts have a merit badge for cinematography, and the Girl Scouts have one for video production.

HOW TO RENT A CAMERA

Renting a camera is a little tricky because you will probably need a credit card, and it can get expensive. Unless you have a fake ID, an adult figure might need to join you at the rental shop. Be forewarned: Going into places that rent cameras can be a little intimidating because the employees cop an attitude that says, "I am in the film biz and you are not." They might also balk at your age. Underneath, though, they are desperate people who wish they were doing what you are doing. Look through them, politely, as you ask about the weekly rate.

If you are having a difficult time locating a place to rent a camera, call a wedding videography business. It is doubtful that they will rent you a camera, but they will at least be able to tell you where they go when they need extras.

THE TRIPOD: ROCK, ROCK, STEADY, STEADY

We work a lot with students, and at first most of them absolutely hate using a tripod. Instead, they go completely handheld, and it shows in a bad way. While tiny rebellions fuel the creativity of filmmaking, this is one place where you want to fall into line. Get a tripod and use it for every shot that does not have any movement. This is probably the number one most preventable mistake that students make.

Good tripods can cost hundreds of dollars, but you can actually get some decent ones for around thirty bucks. Used ones don't go much cheaper, but the same thirty bucks will get you more.

A salesperson is going to tell you that you need a super lightweight, fluid-head, six-foot tripod with wheels that is made especially for video. You don't. For your purposes, you just want a tripod that keeps your camera steady and pans smoothly. Steady means that the legs are solid and that it can hold the weight of your particular camera. A smooth pan allows the camera to rotate back and forth without any jumps or jerks. While a smooth pan is more likely with a video tripod, don't worry if you get a still-picture tripod. Use what you have.

MICROPHONE

Many believe that bad audio is worse than bad video. We still want you to go for the good camera first, but after that your second biggest priority (and second biggest dollar item) is the microphone.

Avoid using an on-camera microphone. It may work for your little brother's birthday party or for your family vacation, but it won't work here. You can never get it close enough to the action. Either your actors will sound like they are miles away from the camera, or the microphone will pick up other sounds in the room. Instead of using your on-camera microphone, you need an external microphone that can go where the action is.

If you are running on a super low budget and cannot afford a microphone other than the on-camera mic, then stay really close to the action. Try to be no more than a few feet from whatever you are shooting.

There are also a few cases where you could get by without an external mic. For example, a closely shot documentary or a short that contains only voice over or music. But for most flicks, you are going to need one external mic.

MIC (MIKE) GATHERING

Don't use the microphone that your friend uses in his band. These "dynamic mics" only pick up sounds that are close to them; they keep out the roar of the crowd. Since they have to be close to one's mouth, they won't work for making movies since you would always see the microphone in the frame.

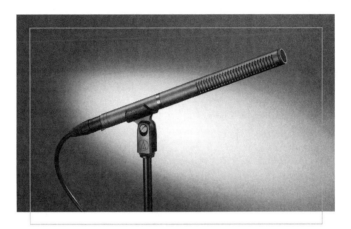

Instead, you will want to look for a shotgun microphone. These microphones are designed to pick up sounds from an actor and yet still remain out of the frame. Shotgun microphones are very directional, meaning that they pick up sound mainly where you point them, and they need power from a battery that is usually located inside the microphone handle but can also come from the camera (called phantom power). While they can transmit their information to the camera wirelessly, they are usually connected to your camera by a cable.

Some productions use little lavaliere mics that can be hidden under an actor's clothing. You have probably seen them clipped on the outside of a person's clothing during a news interview. The little wire that comes off of the microphone can go to the camera, but more often than not it goes to a transmitter that sends the information wirelessly to the camera. We think that a shotgun is your best bet, but we mention lavalieres because you are more likely to have success borrowing these than a shotgun microphone.

In this book, we are going to assume that if you get a lavaliere, you are using a wireless transmitter and receiver system that comes with a lavaliere microphone. If you get a shotgun microphone, then we will assume it is connected to the camera by an actual cable.

HEY MIKE, CAN I BORROW A MIC?

There are a bunch of ways to get a microphone for your shoot. The best option is to convince your teachers that the school needs to have both a shotgun and a wireless microphone if it is ever going to get its film program off the ground. Or, if you personally have the cash and think that you are going to be making other shorts in the future, go ahead and buy a shotgun mic.

Since mics are expensive, with the cheapest one costing in the hundreds, renting or borrowing a mic is your best option. Rental houses will carry both, plus they will throw in some cables. But when borrowing, you will be more likely to scrounge a wireless lavaliere mic since schools and churches tend to have them.

Regardless, don't let the expense of getting a microphone stop you. Besides the camera, it is the one big-ticket item that will make or break your production.

1/8 inch aka Mini Plug

A mini plug is the kind at the end of your iPhone ear buds, and it can also be used on microphones. While most professional cameras use an XLR connector, you are just as likely to have a camera that takes a mini plug for its audio input. If this is the case, Audio Technica makes a special shot gun mic just for you called the ATR-6550, and it costs less than $100! Since it only has a 1-meter cable attached, you can order an extender from Radio Shack.

The audio-in jack (hole) on cameras are notorious for going bad due to the weight of the cord hanging on them. A great way to prevent this is to get a mini plug that turns 90 degrees, called a right angle adapter (Model: 274-372 at Radio Shack).

XLR CABLES

The cable that goes from a shotgun mic to your camera is an XLR cable. You can probably borrow one of these from your drama department. Keep it under twenty-five feet and be sure to test it before you shoot, since XLR cables get abused and can be DOA.

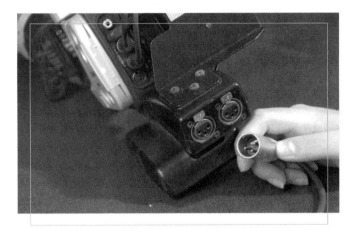

XLR ADAPTER

Most cameras do not have audio inputs that can take XLR connectors. This is a real bummer since you will want to use XLR cables to get good sound. There are three ways to get around this problem. First, buy a camera with XLR inputs. Or, if this is not an option, then get a box that is an adapter from a company like Beachtek. It screws onto the camera and has XLR inputs. You can also buy or make a little inline converter that simply attaches directly to the XLR cable. While cheaper, they tend to be a little rough on your camera and are not nearly as good as the larger and more stable converter boxes. Ultimately, if you can get a camera which comes with XLR inputs, then you don't need to worry about adapters.

BOOM POLE

In order to hold the microphone near your actors, you will need to attach it to a pole. While you can buy this, or rent it for next to nothing, you can also make your own out of a broomstick and some gaffer tape (gaffer tape is explained later in this list). The one thing you will be missing is a shock mount, which attaches to the boom pole and insulates the microphone against extra bumps. If you don't have a shock mount, just be very gentle.

WIND ELIMINATOR

These fuzzy socks go over your shotgun microphone to keep the wind from making a roaring sound. If you are renting your microphone, ask for this as part of an audio package. It's actually called a dead cat. If you are shooting outside, one of these is a must since wind can sound like an oncoming train when recorded onto tape. Some places will also rent you a plastic blimp-looking thing known as a zeppelin. It is a mesh cage that also goes over the microphone. For double protection you can put a larger dead cat over the zeppelin.

HEADPHONES

Borrow the nicest pair you can find. Plug them into the camera, and listen to what is being recorded. Ideally, the person holding the microphone will need to be the one doing the listening, so you may have to buy an extender cable in order for the headphones to reach her. You can also split the audio signal with a cheap splitter from Radio Shack so that the director can hear as well.

CLEAR UV FILTER

This attachment screws onto your lens. It helps your picture a little, but more importantly it keeps the highly expensive lens from getting scratched. If you don't think this is a good idea, compare the cost of a lens (in the thousands) to the cost of a filter (around twenty bucks). Never shoot without one.

DIGITAL VIDEOTAPE/DISCS/ HARD DRIVES

Make sure you buy a name brand, and make sure you buy 50% more than you think you will need. Running out of room feels worse than having no tape at all. Tapes and discs can vary in price, so shop around and buy in bulk; you can always use it later. If you are shooting onto cards, then this is less of an issue, and you can divert these funds to buying a portable hard drive.

BATTERIES

Both your camera and your microphone will need batteries. While you can plug your camera in, going with the battery keeps you from tripping over cords. If you can afford it, buy an extra camera battery and always have one charging while you are shooting. Under all circumstances, make sure you have enough batteries or you risk shutting your production down.

REFLECTORS

Remember, this is one of the top five pieces of equipment that you need to get out of the home video category.

Reflectors allow you to bounce light back onto your scene, and as you will read in the next chapter, they are a great substitute for electric lights. Even if you are using lights, reflectors are super helpful. Professional-grade reflectors are actually not that expensive (under $15 for a silver/white two-sided disc), but you can also make your own really cheaply. Craft stores sell a thing called foam core, and home improvement stores sell big sheets of lightweight material that has a silvery coating on it. When cut into fourths, these home improvement reflectors are really great. Some students like to use the windshield reflectors off of their cars. The silvery ones are always better at reflecting than the foam board, but sometimes this reflection is too much, so it is good to have both on hand.

LIGHTS

There are two routes to take here. If you are short on cash, you can get a fairly decent set of lights at the local hardware store, or you can get a professional kit.

Since lights are really hot, and since they could burn you or catch your set on fire, it is always a good idea to have an adult around when you are using them. We even carry a cheap fire extinguisher with us when we use lights.

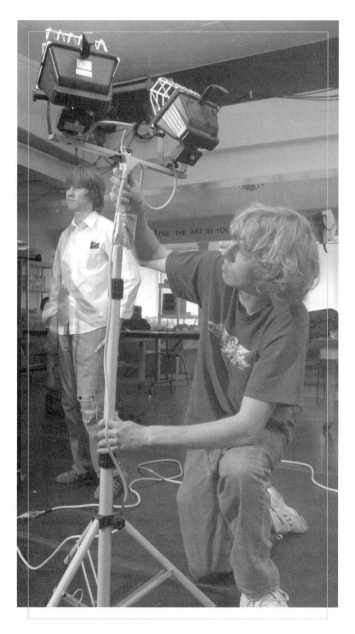

If you go the hardware route, convince mom and dad that they could use the lights around the house and you are set. Hardware stores sell three kinds of lights that could be of use to you. First, there is the good old pie pan light. The metal backing reflects light on the scene, therefore making these lights brighter than they would be otherwise. Be sure never to put a light bulb in the socket with a higher wattage than the socket is rated for.

Another type of light is a standard work light. These are neat because they sometimes come with a stand. Both the work lights and the pie pans will probably need some sort of diffusion, so don't just plug and go. Read the next chapter first.

Hardware stores also sell really cheap handheld fluorescent lights. Lighting experts don't like fluorescents because they flicker, are a little green, and can change color over time. We say go ahead and give them a try. You probably won't be able to notice the difference, although you'll probably need to turn on your camera's manual white balance. These lights don't get as hot as pie pans or work lights, and they are already somewhat diffuse. If you can get one with a frosted cover, even better. They are so cheap that you might want to buy a few.

You may be lucky enough to acquire a professional lighting kit. These kits are a bit expensive, and we would rather you first spend your money on a camera, microphone, and pizza for the crew, so don't make this a first priority. Pro lighting kits usually come with stands, lights, and barndoors to help you manipulate the light. See the next chapter for a discussion of barndoors.

You may be able to borrow some lights from a school drama department, but often these are way too bright for what you are doing, unless you are shooting outside. They also get really hot and require a lot of electricity.

You might also think about shooting right on a school's stage or under the football field lights. More about this in the next chapter.

BLACK PLASTIC AND BLUE TAPE

When shooting inside, the sunlight from the windows looks much different than light from light bulbs. Video is notorious for making ugly images when you combine the two. So get rid of the sun. In order to block out the windows, you can buy black plastic in rolls from Home Depot in the paint section, and then cut it to the size of the windows you are covering. Use blue painters tape to hang the plastic as it is designed to be nice to paint. (Another way that the pros deal with this is to put gels in front of the lights that make the light the color of the sun.)

BLACK FOIL

Like heavy-duty aluminum foil, black foil attaches to your lights and will help you direct light where you want it. It's black so that it doesn't cause reflections. Be careful; it gets really hot.

ELECTRICAL CORD

Most homes have an extension cord lying around, which will usually be fine to power your monitor, your battery chargers, or your camera, but it might not be thick enough to carry the current generated by lights. If you are doing a lot of lighting, try to get a thicker and more heavy-duty extension cord. Best of all, get an adult to help you make this decision. It's better than burning down the house.

SURGE PROTECTOR

We like to use surge protectors because they will shut off when too much current comes through their wires. It is better to stop the production because of an electrical problem than an electrical fire. We don't mean to scare you. Actually, the room's circuit breaker will probably shut you down before a fire starts. Regardless, before using massive amounts of electricity, find an adult to sign off on what you are doing.

GLOVES

Lights get really hot. Don't turn on the lights until you have these.

WHITE BALANCE CARD

You need something that is white which you can use to set the white balance on your camera. A white shirt will do, even if someone is wearing it, but a small, dedicated piece of poster board is best. You can also buy these relatively cheaply. More about this in the next chapter.

MONITOR

Have a television on the set to which you can connect your camera. The director can then look at the shot framed just like it is framed in the camera. You will need a long RCA (yellow, red, white) cord to attach your camera to the television. Actually, you just need to run the yellow out from the camera to yellow in on your TV. There is nothing special about yellow. You just need a single long RCA cord from Radio Shack of any color, as long as you connect the yellow out and yellow in. You can put two RCA cords together with a little barrel adapter.

GAFFER TAPE

A less sticky cousin of duct tape, this is great for securing anything on the set, especially cables onto the floor so that people don't trip. Taping down cords is time consuming at first, but really worth it when you save your camera as well as your friend's tibia.

DIFFUSION

You use this to soften harsh light. Lots of items can be used as diffusion: a frosted shower curtain, a white bed sheet, a white air-conditioning filter, actual diffusion paper, baking paper. A school drama department may have some diffusion paper. The biggest catch is that diffusion is often used around lights, and lights mean fire. Be careful.

STABILIZER

Okay, so there are times when you won't use a tripod. When this happens, camera stabilizers allow you to go handheld with confidence. They come in over-the-shoulder models as well as upright models. You will see pictures of them throughout this book.

DOLLY

A dolly is just something with wheels on it. Since dolly shots can make your movie look pretty cool, this may be the one thing off of the big budget list that you should look for. A lot of people use wheelchairs because they roll smoothly and fit through doorways. Think also about using skateboards, an AV cart from school, or your kid sister's wagon. Scavenge some lumber to put on the ground so they roll smoothly. You can also rent dollies if there is a gear rental place in your town.

SANDBAGS

These help to hold down stands and keep them from getting knocked over. Look to your school for this.

STANDS

Stands come in handy in lots of situations from lighting to audio. Maybe your friend's garage band has a microphone stand. Professional stands are often called C-stands, and your theater department just might have these. If you are using stands, you also need sandbags.

EXTRA LENSES

Most digital video cameras do not have a removable lens. If yours does, however, think about renting a wide-angle lens. If your camera does not have a removable lens (or even if it does), then there are lens attachments that will convert your lens to a wide angle. A wide-angle lens really helps when shooting in tight spaces. There are also fish-eye lenses as well as fish-eye attachments that will give your piece the gnarly skateboard feel.

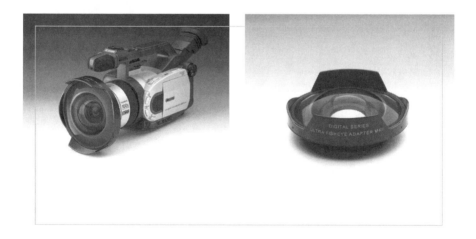

POLARIZING FILTER

If you are shooting outside a lot, a polarizing filter cuts down the glare and makes the blue sky beautiful. Your images will pop, but this is a $60 expense you can do without. Make sure the filter you get is specifically designed for digital video.

DIGITAL STILL CAMERA

When it comes time to publicize your film, or better yet, when you make it big, you are going to need some pictures of your film. While you could use still frames from your movie, digital video does not have the resolution to make high quality prints. The print industry usually wants digital stills to be 300 dots per inch (dpi), and if you are shooting 720 lines of horizontal resolution, that means you could only print a high quality image that is 2.4 inches high. So, it is better to use a high-resolution digital still camera to capture your production stills.

JIB ARM

If money is no concern, and if you really, really, really want your movie to look awesome, rent a jib arm. This device allows you to take your camera from ten or more feet off the ground down to eye level or more. The shots are really smooth and look very pro.

THE LISTS:

Low Budget List

Camera

Tripod

Reflector/Shine Board

Shotgun Microphone

Microphone Batteries

Boom Pole

XLR Cable or Mini Plug Extender Cable

Mini-DV Tape or Discs

Black Plastic

Blue Tape

Big Budget List

Camera

Extra Camera Batteries

Tripod

Extension Cord

Shotgun Microphone

Wireless Microphone

Microphone Batteries

XLR Cable

XLR Converter

Boom Pole

Windscreen

Camera Stabilizer

Lighting Kit

Black Foil

Doorway Dolly

Track Dolly

Sandbags

C Stands

Diffusion

Scrims

Reflectors

Extra lenses

Monitor

Long Cord for Monitor

Clear Filter

Polarizing Filter

Digital Still Camera

Jib Arm

RESHOOT

Equipment: Getting the whole package.

▶ Just a camera isn't enough, though a good one helps, and "three-chip" rules.

▶ Tripod – find good "sticks" and use them.

▶ Shotgun Mic – on-camera mics are good for birthday parties.

▶ Reflector – like lights, but cheaper.

▶ Monitor – see what you're doing.

▶ Choose the equipment list that fits your budget.

CHAPTER

9

GETTING PRETTY
PICTURES

U-G-L-Y, DO YOU HAVE AN ALIBI?

You probably have never seen an ugly film. You have seen stupid films, you have seen poorly acted films, and you have seen boring films. But were they ugly? Probably not because filmmaking is a visual art form, and, as a result, ugly films don't make it to the big screen. Your first goal in this project is to make your film "not ugly," which is just another way of saying you need to meet some basic expectations to be taken seriously. Once your short is "not ugly," then and only then should you make it beautiful. We are going to show you how to do both by concentrating on two aspects of filmmaking: lighting and composition.

Just in case you don't have time to read the rest of this chapter, here are eight hints to making your short "not ugly." If you want to make your short look good, you will have to read the chapter. Sorry.

Dos
1. Use a tripod.
2. Use a variety of camera angles and heights.
3. Shoot in locations that are visually interesting.
4. Fill the frame with something interesting.

Don'ts
5. Do NOT use autofocus.
6. Do NOT use zoom.
7. Do NOT put every actor in the middle of the screen.
8. Do NOT shoot with strong light behind or above your characters.

PART ONE: LIGHTING

Your eye is much better than a camera at picking up color and light, so you will need to help your camera along. This is the "not ugly" part. You need to light a scene evenly enough so that all parts of the frame look good. Once you have done this, you can then use lighting to make your movie beautiful by setting mood, creating depth, and experimenting with color.

BEFORE YOU PLUG IN THE LIGHTS,
OR WHAT TO DO IF YOU DON'T PLUG IN THE LIGHTS

Although we are going to teach you to use lights, we first want you to consider not using them. You are a beginning filmmaker, and your easiest and cheapest option may be to avoid them. This does not mean that you get to ignore lighting altogether, it just means you are not going to plug anything into the wall at first. If this method works for you, then run with it. In the end, the tricks you use and the choices you make without lights will be helpful even if you do end up plugging in.

In addition to running without lights, we want you to start off by using the automatic setting on your camera. This means that you are letting the little computer in your camera decide what aperture setting to use and what white balance to use. Be careful: You still want control of the focus. TURN OFF AUTOFOCUS. :-@

FIRST, USE A MONITOR

In order to see the bright and dark areas, use a monitor. It will show you what the camera is seeing. Not only does this help with lighting, it also gives you an advantage in the focusing and framing departments.

While the pros use special monitors, all you need is a TV, a long cord to go from your camera to the TV, and a friend to hold the cord. The cord is usually like the one you find going from a DVD player to a TV. You know, the yellow, white, and red cables. Just connect yellow out to yellow in.

Your friend who is holding the cable is called a grip or PA, and his job is to keep people from tripping over the cord thereby causing injury to them and the camera. If your tripod is going to be in one place for most of the day or the whole shoot, use gaffer tape to secure the cords.

SECOND, TAKE TIME TO CHOOSE YOUR LOCATION WISELY

So now you are on your big shoot with no lights plugged in, automatic mode engaged, and a monitor attached. Don't get too comfortable because while your camera is smart, it is also limited. Sure, it can determine the average amount of light in a frame and adjust itself appropriately. But sometimes it can't adjust for the really bright and the really dark spots at the same time. It has a small range of brightness to darkness in which it can operate. If you have something really bright and something really dark, the camera does not know what to do, and one of these areas will lose all detail. It will become totally white or totally black.

Your job is to look for the areas where the image is too bright or too dark, then fix these problems. The bright areas may require you to change locations or camera angle, while the dark areas can be solved with reflectors (or lights if you have them).

If direct sunlight is too harsh, move to the shadows. If shadows are too dark compared to the background, move to the sunlit areas. If neither one will do, put your actor in the shadows and frame her so that the sunlit background is out of frame. Or shoot later in the day when sunlight isn't so harsh.

Video cameras cannot handle BOTH the bright truck and the person in the shadows at the same time.

THIRD, USE REFLECTORS

It's there, we promise. At first, you may not see the shadows and dark spots since your brain is so accustomed to filtering out this kind of stuff. For example, look at someone's neck. If you're in a room with overhead lighting, his or her neck is bound to be in the shadows.

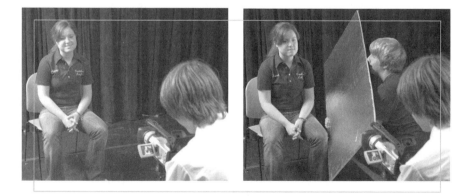

The way to fill in the dark areas is to make or buy a reflector (of course you could use lights too, but we will get to that later). Use the reflector to take what light already exists and put it back onto your scene. Sometimes you will be throwing it onto your actor's face, and other times you will be throwing it on the background.

Reflected light is great because it is the same type and color of light as that which you are already using. Moreover, it is a little less bright than your primary light. Think perfume. Use none at all and you might get by. A whiff of it will take you from average to beautiful. Too much and you have to roll down the windows.

While you can purchase a handy-dandy professional, collapsing reflector, you can also make your own. Just get a piece of white foam core from a craft store or go to a hardware store and get a foam board that has a foil backing. Even white poster board or a windshield reflector can do in a pinch.

As an experiment, try this. No really, try this. Don't just read about it. Take your camera and plug it into a television set. Find a place with overhead lighting and frame your friend from the waist up. Do you see the shadows? Maybe not at first, but once you point that reflector at her chin you will get it, that nice whiff of perfume. You probably will want another friend to help out here so that you can watch the monitor. Get used to calling the shots.

Remember that reflectors were in our top five list of pieces of equipment that you should have beyond your camera. Use them frequently to fill in the light on your subjects.

FOURTH, USE BLACK PLASTIC AND BLUE TAPE

When shooting inside, windows let in a lot of light. Not only is it usually too bright, it also is a different kind (or color) of light than light bulbs. Since you cannot over-power the sun, get rid of it. Using painters tape (often blue), which is designed not to strip paint off of walls, hang some black painters plastic on the windows. Then frame your shots such that no windows are in the frame. Move furniture if you have too. You can bypass this all together by shooting at night.

FIFTH, DON'T MIX DIFFERENT TYPES OF LIGHT

Avoid mixing fluorescent bulbs and regular old light bulbs. Sunlight and light bulbs are also a bad combo. We will tell you some ways to get around this in the latter part of this chapter, but for now avoid the combination. Here is why.

A filmmaker's nightmare. This room would be very difficult to light.

Sunlight is a lot different than fluorescent light, which is a lot different than incandescent light. Even though we think of them all as generally white, they are not. When you have two different colored lights in a shot, it is both distracting and can actually lead to some bad coloring. So, try to use all one of one kind of light.

Just ask a physics or chemistry teacher for a spectrometer. Remember those? You used them in colored flame experiments or with neon tubes. Check out a fluorescent light and then an incandescent light bulb. (Forget checking out the sun or you will go blind. Galileo went blind from looking at the sun and he never made a film in his life.) The two bulbs will look different in the spectroscope.

While white light is made of a bunch of other colors, some light that we call white does not actually have all the colors in it. On the flip side, fluorescents actually have an excess of green. Cameras notice these differences while our eyes and brain filter them out.

FROM AUTOMATIC TO FIVE SPEED
So far we have encouraged you to go with no lights and to use the automatic features of your camera. Buckle your seatbelts.

Earlier in this book we asked which you would choose, a camera or a car? What if your parents offered you both? Having already picked out the camera, which car would you choose: A minivan with an automatic transmission, or a sports car with five-speed manual transmission?

Slow down. Don't let go of the minivan just yet. Automatics are good because they allow you to ignore switching gears, thereby letting you focus on good driving practices. We are making an analogy here, just in case you missed it. Going automatic on your camera lets you focus on other things like acting.

Note: If your parents have a mini van, use it. They make for great production vehicles as they can carry your gear and your crew!

Okay, now let go of the minivan. Why did you choose the sports car? Why do sports cars come with manual transmissions? You have more control. It can do things that a minivan can't. Most important to our little analogy, you can pass others at will.

Choose a Ferrari over the minivan, then you can use it in your short.

FIRST GEAR: ZEBRA BARS

Most cameras have a zebra setting which highlights overly bright areas. You can use this in conjunction with the next few gears in order to get a good picture. Reduce the number of zebra bars and your picture will look better.

SECOND GEAR: SHUTTER SPEED

Still cameras that use film actually have a shutter that opens and closes, and with these cameras, the shutter speed measures how long the shutter stays open. While digital cameras don't actually open and close a shutter, they still take pictures at a speed as if they were opening and closing, so the word "shutter speed" is still used.

The truth of the matter is that you seldom will change shutter speed, but there are times when it is useful to know how.

The safe setting for shutter speed is 1/60 of a second. Leave the "shutter" open for longer than this and images start to blur (1/30 is actually a longer time period that 1/60, just like 1/2 is bigger than 1/8 in math, so 1/30 is more likely to blur than 1/60). However, if you are in a low light situation without a lot of movement, you might choose to go to 1/30. Going even lower (like 1/15 or 1/8) could produce a dreamy effect that you might be able to use in a cool way. Don't overuse it, or dreams become a film festival judge's nightmare.

You also can increase the shutter speed. This might be necessary if you are trying to manipulate depth of field (see aperture), but really fast shutter speed looks too digital. Be careful and intentional with shutter speed.

You can adjust the shutter speed in two ways. One option is a setting which gives you shutter priority. You just change the shutter speed while the camera fixes everything else. The second way is to go completely manual, meaning that you have control of everything on the camera. This can be a little dangerous since changing the shutter speed in one direction can affect what you need to do with the aperture.

For most of your shooting, you will use 1/60 of a second shutter speed. It is the aperture that you will adjust to change the amount of light comes in.

THIRD GEAR: APERTURE, F-STOP, IRIS

Like shutter speed, the aperture setting (or f-stop) determines how much light gets into your camera. While shutter speed uses time, aperture uses space. It opens up the lens wider to get more light and closes it tighter to get less light. Just like the shutter speed, you can control the aperture in manual mode, or you can use the aperture priority setting.

Changing the aperture can do a few things. First, it can lighten or darken your picture. Set the zebra bars on and the shutter speed to 1/60. Now use the aperture to decrease or increase the light until your main subject looks good. By decreasing the f-stop (the technical word for the aperture setting) you will be opening up the iris (eye) of the camera bigger and letting more light in. Other parts of the scene may be a little dark or bright, but in this stage you are adjusting for the actor. Once the actor is properly lit, then you can add and remove light as discussed earlier.

There are other things you can do with the iris. If you have a heaven scene that you wanted to make really bright, then let in a lot of light by decreasing the f-stop, which means that you are opening the iris. Or if you have a scene that is spooky or romantic, you might darken it by increasing the f-stop.

The aperture also affects depth of field. A lot of film folks complain about video because it has so much depth of field, meaning that everything is in focus. But you can use the aperture to reduce depth of field. This means that you are creating a picture where your subject is in focus but the background is out of focus. Your picture now has dimension and your short film looks better.

To understand this, put your finger as close to your face as you can while still being able to focus on it. The wall on the other side of the room is out of focus. Now focus on the other side of the room and your finger will drop out of focus.

We think that you should try to create a shallow depth of field at least once in your short. Make sure to practice it a bunch before the shoot using the TV-as-monitor method. Here is what you do.

First, make sure your subject is far away from the background.

Next zoom in as much as possible on your subject and get as close to your subject as possible. Realize though, that these two suggestions are hard to do at the same time.

For example, if you zoom in, then you start to see less and less in your picture. Where you used to see a car and a driver, now you just see the driver. What are you going to do if you wanted to see the whole car, but are trying to keep the camera at maximum zoom? The answer is to move the camera back. At this point you are canceling out the shallow focus benefits of the zoom.

Or to look at it another way, if you are really close to your subject, you cannot see all of what you want to see, so without moving the camera you zoom out, thereby canceling the benefit of being close to the subject.

If you want a lot of things in your picture, it is harder to get a shallow depth of field.

The final hint is to make the f-stop as low as it can go, which really means making the iris as big as it can get. If this ends up letting in too much light, most cameras have a built in ND filter (neutral density), which will allow you to make the overall scene darker.

FOURTH GEAR: WHITE BALANCE

White balancing is a way of telling the camera, "here is what the color white is supposed to look like with these particular lights." This is one area where our eye/brain combo is not as good as the camera/computer combo. We may think that the white light from fluorescents is pretty similar to the white light from a desk lamp, but a camera will see them as different. A white shirt in one will look yellow in another. If you can avoid it, don't mix different types of light in the same scene. The camera will choose one as the dominant light, and as a result, the other one will look weird.

Actually, the auto white balance works pretty well on most cameras. Feel free to use it. But if you want to make your colors more consistent, try the manual white balance. If you don't, then when the light in a room changes, your camera will change and try to compensate. Whites will change to dull yellow or pale blue during the middle of the scene.

In order to set the white balance, just put something white in place of your actors, push the manual white balance button, and your camera will color correct for the lights at hand. You can get professional white balance cards, or you can borrow a piece of white paper from a copying machine.

In order to make your short unique, and possibly beautiful, try white balancing with something that is off-white. Professional white balance cards often come with a variety of whites that can help to make your film look warmer. They are fairly inexpensive and worth it if your school is footing the bill for your production.

There is one big danger with using manual white balance and that is forgetting to reset it when the light changes. Of course, if you are using a monitor you will be able to tell when your actor's skin looks blue.

FIFTH GEAR: PROGRESSIVE SCAN

Some think that video is ugly when compared to film. It looks too smooth and continuous, whereas film has a little bit of choppiness to it. As moviegoers we have come to love that little bit of subconscious choppiness.

Traditionally, video is interlaced, which means that at any given moment you are actually seeing half of now and half of the past 1/60 a second. While you would think interlaced video makes for choppy, it actually makes for smoothie. "Smoothie" is not a word commonly used in a film class. Use it at Dairy Queen instead.

The smoothness of video is ugly. If you can get progressive scan or "one frame at a time scan," then your video will look more like film. The catch: It works better with a lot of light.

PLUGGING IN THE LIGHTS

Lighting is an art form in and of itself. Get it right and you are in a totally new class of filmmakers. Get it wrong and you would have been better off without it.

We think you can do it, but it definitely takes practice, a larger crew, more time to set up, and a little bit of tenacity on your behalf. We'll let you make the call. We also have to remind you, lights are hot and they can burn your skin and cause fires. Don't bring your film career to an early end by burning down your house.

As you begin to play with lighting, avoid locations where the sun or any other really bright light is the main lighting source. Most likely your lights will not be able to compete, so you will have to get them closer to the subject. Often this ends up being too close, and the audience can then tell you are using artificial lighting. Instead, try the reflector method mentioned earlier.

To succeed when you first try lighting, shoot at night or in dark rooms, and let your light source be the primary giver of light. If at all possible, try to use diffuse light, which we discuss below. It is easier for beginners to work with.

Lighting could take up a whole book, so we have boiled it down.

Rule number 1: Start with your main character, and then light the rest of the scene.

Rule number 2: Manipulate where you throw the light, almost always bounce it off a wall.

Rule number 3: Diffuse your lights; the easiest way is to bounce off of a wall.

Rule number 4: Use lights to create depth.

Rule number 5: Use lights to create mood.

Rule number 6: Get creative.

START WITH YOUR ACTION

Your first goal is to light your main character or whatever is important in your scene. Then, just as we discussed in the no-light section, you should look into the monitor for dark and bright spots elsewhere. Remember to let the camera's zebra function help you find the bright spots.

When given an image, our eyes tend to gravitate toward both faces and things that are bright. Try not to have items in your image that are far brighter than an actor or an actor's face.

THROW YOUR LIGHT AROUND

The problem with light is that it tends to spread out and go places you don't want it to go. Another problem with light is that it adds up.

Say that you already have light on your main character, and now you are trying to light the background. If any of the background lighting spills onto your main character, then he or she will get even brighter.

In order to prevent this, professional lighting kits have what are called barn doors. Barn doors are simply little pieces of metal that fold over the light to keep it from spilling left, right, up, or down. If your lighting kit does not have these, then you can have a production assistant hold a piece of foamboard to where it blocks the unwanted spillage. Don't get too close to the light with the foamcore as it could catch fire. Finally, you can use heavy-duty black aluminum foil on the light and just shape it in a way that directs the light. Since fire is also a possibility here, it is best to have an adult around to take the heat when you burn down the location.

Helpful hint: Pay attention to an interview in a professional documentary and you will see the following method used. Keep your main characters from getting too close to what is behind them (if possible). Then, when you shine light on them from an angle, the shadows will be off in never-never land out of frame. You can now light the background with a light from a different angle. If instead they were leaning against a wall, the shadows would be obvious on the wall, and the two lights would start to add up, making the background brighter than your subject.

DIFFUSION

The way to reduce the intensity of light as well as soften it is to diffuse it. This is often done by placing some sort of opaque material between the light and your subject. The light casts less shadows and seems less harsh. If you are shooting a suspense thriller, then you may not want to use diffusion. But otherwise, diffusion is often the beginning filmmaker's best friend.

You can buy diffusion material at camera stores or at theater supply stores. Check with the tech folks in your drama department. Or, you can hold a frosted shower curtain or a white air conditioning filter in front of a light. An even simpler option is to bounce light off of a ceiling, wall, or piece of foam core. What used to be light coming from a bulb is now light coming from a big wall. If your shots are too bright, the bounce method is a great solution. Finally, some professional light kits like the Lowel Rifa Light come with special diffusion attachments.

Did we mention that lights can create fire?

This professional Rifa light from Lowel has a diffuser attached to the light box.

USE LIGHT TO CREATE DEPTH: THREE-POINT LIGHTING

In film school, your first lighting lecture will be about three-point lighting. We mention three-point lighting because it can make your flick look really cool. The technique itself takes a lot of practice, so if three-point lighting does not work for you, then scrap it. At the same time, if you have a really responsible friend to whom you can give this job, it may make your film notably well lit. Also, given the lights that you have available to you, three-point lighting will work better for shots that don't require the camera to move or the actors to move.

The basic idea of three-point lighting is to hit your main action with light from one angle. This light, called a key light, is usually positioned both 45 degrees from the ground and 45 degrees to the side of the actors.

A second, softer light is used from the other side of the actors, and it serves to fill in some of the shadows. With both the key light and the fill light, try to keep them from hitting the part of the wall behind the actors that is in the frame. If you cannot keep them from hitting the wall, use barndoors or a piece of foamcore.

Finally, hit the actor from behind and above with a light called a kicker. It puts a nice little ring of light on the actors head and serves to distinguish the actor from the background.

If all you have is one or no lights, you can still make three-point lighting work by using whatever natural light you have available and then using shine boards to make up the other three.

Three-point lighting will make your movie look like other professionally shot movies. It also gives dimension to a scene. Your real world is three-dimensional and the movie screen is two-dimensional, so any way you that you can find to make your shots seem more three-dimensional is a good thing.

LIGHT IS NOT LINEAR

If you move a light twice as close to subject, it is four times as bright due to a little thing called the inverse square law that you will study in physics. Be prepared to move lights around, and realize that a little change can make a big difference.

SETTING THE MOOD

Use more light or less light or colored lights to set mood. Another option is to make some cool patterns on the wall by cutting out shapes in foam core and placing it in front of a light (called a cookie). When you zoom way in, these patterns make the wall behind your character look cool. They can even be made to look like a window frame at night.

Try shining lights up at your characters' faces. It is a classic way to make them look sinister. Experiment with a variety of different light angles to create cool shadows both on your characters and the set.

GET CREATIVE

Make your set right on the school's stage. Maybe even try to piggy back on a big performance while the lighting is still set and someone remembers how to control it. What the heck, borrow their set before they strike it. Volunteer to strike it. A huge plus is that you will be able to control sound. Also, props and other theater gear are probably close at hand.

If you do shoot on stage, keep your shots tight and no one will be able to tell. Also, don't forget to white balance because some productions use some pretty funky lighting.

Your school might also have a football field, parking lot, or a tennis court with night lights. These are often really bright and make some beautiful light. A few reflectors might be needed since the lights are overhead. Again, keep the shots tight and no one will see the net. In basketball you want the shots to be nothing but net. Here you want the shot to be everything but the net.

PART TWO: COMPOSITION OR FRAMING

There are hundreds of framing techniques — way too many to be discussed in this book and way too many to include in your movie. But there are a few basic principles that will keep your film from looking ugly. There are also a few techniques that can help your film to look good.

FRAMING UGLIES

Ugly framing is the kind you see in the mirror every morning. Don't be insulted. What we mean is that when a character's face or upper body is perfectly centered on the screen, it is just too simple. Many viewers find it plain and boring. You've got lots of real estate. Explore it.

The technical term for the empty space above a character is "head room." As you direct your film, be ready to tell your camera operator to watch the head room.

Poor Composition: His head is in the middle of the screen and overwhelmed by an irrelevant background.

Good Composition. He occupies a lot more of the screen and is positioned off center.

16:9 VS. 4:3

16:9 is pronounced "sixteen nine" and is the standard in HD television. It refers to the ratio of horizontal to vertical pixels, with 16:9 looking more rectangular than the square 4:3. Older cameras shoot in SD which is in 4:3 , although almost all have the option to fake 16:9. Faking 16:9 can get really complicated in the editing studio, but it is worth it. There are two ways to do it: anamorphic or letter box. Anamorphic is better in the end, but much more complicated. Choose your poison, but never shoot in 4:3.

NO SHAKY SHAKY

Another really common mistake is shooting with a shaky camera. No matter what kind of camera you have acquired to shoot your movie, it is guaranteed to have a little hole on the bottom for a tripod to screw into. You must use it. It is so tempting and easy to just forget the tripod and go handheld. But the problem is that you won't notice that the camera is shaky because you are shaking with it. Then when you go to show it on the big screen your audience will barf — both metaphorically and literally.

You may think we are exaggerating since you survived *Blair Witch*, but we are not exaggerating. During the *Blair Witch* phenomenon, a local theater in our town reported an average of one person a day throwing up in the theater. Now that is ugly, especially if you work there.

An even better reason to use a tripod is that when a camera shakes unnaturally, it tends to throw movie watchers out of the movie-watching experience. They think, "Did somebody bump the camera?" When you distract the viewer like this, she sits outside of your work rather than inside it. The viewer's perceived position with respect to your piece is important to keep in mind with every aspect of your movie making.

Our students complain about how silly a small camera looks on a tripod. That is because they never see the teeming masses of camcorder-owning sports moms and dads using tripods. Newsflash: The teeming masses are not filmmakers. You are. You can't afford to be embarrassed about what you are doing. Get over it. Plus, which would you rather look good: you or the movie?

Be aware that there are groups of filmmakers who believe that handheld is the only way to go. We think the best bet for your money is to try and avoid it unless the script motivates it.

It is actually okay to go without a tripod, but if you do, make sure that you use a shoulder-braced stabilizer or some other sort of stabilizer. The real problem comes when you hold the camera with just your hand.

NO ZOOM ZOOM

Don't use the zoom to simulate motion of the camera. Our eyes don't zoom. Instead, our legs walk somewhere and our eyes come along for the ride. Zooms are unnatural, and while your family (and their eyes) won't walk out of your premiere because you used zoom, the reviewer at the film festival may put your demo tape in the ugly pile. You can use zoom to set up your framing; just don't use it while the camera is rolling. One exception to this rule is the slow zoom used for dramatic effect. Usually these are so slow that they can barely be detected. Or a really fast zoom can be used to stylize a movie.

JUST SAY NO TO AUTOFOCUS

Likewise, you can use autofocus to set up a shot, but never use it during a shot. Autofocus has a mind of its own and will do what it wants when it wants, causing your perfectly acted scene to suddenly go out of focus. Cut.

A CONVERSATION ABOUT CONVERSATIONS

Time for another movie break. Any movie you want. Pay attention to a scene in which there is a conversation between two people, or aliens, or dogs. Rewind and watch the conversation three or four times. Don't just study it; Enjoy it because it will be the last time you ever watch a conversation the same way again.

If you are shooting conversations, "don't cross the axis." Simply stated, if you draw an imaginary line (the axis) between two characters who are having a conversation, then you should always keep the camera on one side of that line or the other. Don't mix it up. If you are not sure why, whip out a camera and give this a try. Cross the axis. Once you edit the footage you will immediately see the problem. It tends to confuse the viewer as the characters are on the same side of the screen in both shots.

Of course, you can break this rule and any rule we suggest. But in most movies the axis does not get crossed. The next movie you watch will have a conversation scene in it, and we can almost guarantee you the price of this book that the filmmaker will not have crossed the axis during the conversation.

A conversation.

Camera A

Camera B

Camera A

Camera c

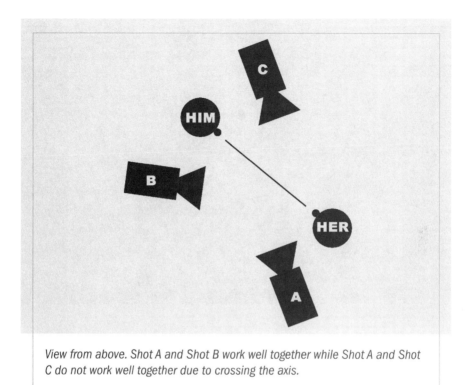

View from above. Shot A and Shot B work well together while Shot A and Shot C do not work well together due to crossing the axis.

In the end, if you follow the framing steps listed so far, then your movie will be "not ugly." Congratulations. Seriously. You are way ahead of the competition. In fact, be ready to shoot most of your movie like this. But, and this is a big but, to make your movie beautiful, you need to throw in some moving shots as well as a variety of other framing techniques.

COMPOSITION: THE ART

In order for your short to look interesting, you need to include a variety of camera angles, camera movements, and composition.

CAMERA ANGLES

Mix it up. Put your camera up high and down low. Shoot from a ladder. When shooting down low, get a little kid's bean bag or a pile of dirty laundry to stabilize your camera. Shoot at an angle. Shoot through a window, behind some bushes at a mirror, or at a TV screen. Look up at a character and he will seem domineering. Look down at a character and he will seem small. Use the camera angle as a way

to show the point of view of a character. Your imagination is the limit here. This little paragraph is really important to your short. Read it again.

Spend a day just practicing different camera angles. The more you do this, the better you will be. Pick a location, shoot it a bunch of different ways. Then go home and watch what you shot. You will quickly see that some of it looks really bad, and some of it looks interesting.

MOVING SHOTS

There are three ways that you as a beginning filmmaker can create moving shots: using the head on the tripod, pushing a dolly (which is a fancy name for a cart with wheels for your camera) or going handheld with a stabilizer.

Moving shots add so much to the production value of your short not only because they just look great, but also because so many other filmmakers don't do them. Give one a try and you will see what we mean.

TRIPOD HEAD MOVEMENT

A left/right rotation of the camera is called a "pan" and can be used to follow motion or to show a scene that is too big to be included in one frame. Be sure that your tripod is level when doing a pan or else the camera will also be going up and down as it moves left and right. Some tripods have a leveling bubble on them, but if not you can carry a little mini-level which you can buy at a hardware store.

An up/down rotation is called a "tilt" and is used to explore the height of things from humans to buildings. It can also be used to follow something falling through the air like a bungee jumper.

A third type of rotation is a little less common, probably because it is not something the human head does easily. We shake our head yes (a tilt) and no (a pan) but we seldom rotate our face clockwise or counterclockwise. You are getting pretty funky if you use this shot plus it can discombobulate viewers. Use it sparingly.

THE DOLLY

Another way to add motion to your film is put your camera and tripod onto or into something with wheels, aka a dolly. Since humans lurch when they walk, dolly motion looks smoother than handheld motion. You can use a wheelchair, a grocery cart, a skateboard, a car, or a cloned sheep. But be careful. You can drop your camera, or worse yet, your camera operator. If you have a friend in shop class who is looking for a project, have him or her build a really cool track dolly out of plastic pipe and plywood.

It is really worth the effort to try and get a dolly shot in your film.

HANDHELD

The easiest and cheapest way to add motion is to go handheld. The problem is that smaller cameras tend to bounce around a lot because they have less mass (thank you, Mr. Newton), so you must find a way to stabilize them. Inexpensive stabilizers can be bought for around $100. They attach to the tripod and rest against your shoulder for stability. An even cheaper one can be built for around $20. Ultimately, if you have to shoot handheld without a stabilizer, so be it. Just be really steady and don't drink a lot of caffeine on the day you shoot.

When might you go handheld? When either the shakiness adds to the shot or the tripod and dolly won't work. For example, you have a character who is nervously

walking through the woods and you want to show his point of view (POV). Cut to the handheld shot. A little shakiness would actually be realistic here because he is walking. Or, if in this same scene you want to follow him from behind as he walks through the woods you would have to go handheld because a wheelchair dolly or skateboard could not roll down the trail. Donnie Darko has a really cool, long shot where the camera moves down a school hallway full of people and lockers. You would need to go handheld to do this kind of shot, and a stabilizer would really help.

When the time comes to go handheld, do it sparingly and intentionally.

THE JIB ARM

If money is no object, rent a jib arm. A local rental house in our town rents them for $100 a day, which may seem steep, but the shots you get are really worth it. The camera seems to glide through the air as you pull it through a three-dimensional camera move. We have to warn you, though, these things are addictive.

SOME FINAL HINTS

Look at the whole frame. Fill it with something interesting, or fill it with nothing. But be sure that you are consciously doing something or nothing with it. Next, in addition to what is on your shotboard, try to get the following: a wide shot, a medium shot, and a close-up shot for every scene you do. This will guarantee that when you get to the editing room, you will have enough extra shots to tell the story. Also, get a lot of extra footage of the scene from different angles and of different objects in the scene. These different shots can save you when your favorite shot has a glitch in it or if you decide to tell the story a little differently in the editing room.

If your camera can take extra lenses, it might be worth renting one for a day. Few beginning filmmakers use wide-angle lenses. If you do, then your short may look a little different than the rest of the pile. Plus you can shoot in small spaces. You can get lenses that replace your cameras lens, or ones that screw on to your cameras lens.

You can learn even more camera moves by checking out *Setting Up Your Shots: Great Camera Moves Every Filmmaker Should Know* by Jeremy Vineyard and Jose Cruz.

RESHOOT
Lighting and framing: Looking good.

▸ Do use a tripod, a variety of angles, cool locations, and thoughtful framing.
▸ Don't use auto-focus, zooms, centered actors, or crossed axis.
▸ Stay unplugged if possible.
▸ Use a monitor to check for shadows and shine boards to fill them in.
▸ Avoid mixing light sources.
▸ Know how to drive your camera both as a manual and an automatic.
▸ If you plug in, use diffused light, usually by bouncing light off of walls.
▸ Manipulate light to manipulate mood.
▸ Include one shot with a short depth of field.

CHAPTER

10

GETTING GOOD
SOUND

People don't just watch movies; they listen to them too. And while good sound seldom gets noticed (with the exception of an awesome sound-track), it is bad sound that will identify your work as a beginner piece. If your audio stinks, you might as well sew a scarlet "A" onto your director's shirt (the A stands for amateur).[2] This chapter deals with what you will have to do to get good sound while you are shooting. Better yet, this chapter lists what you are going to ask someone else to do during the shoot.

We are a little worried you just skimmed the last paragraph, so we are going to reiterate. "Bad audio" is a synonym for "home video." You are not home video. Look, this chapter is short. Please read it carefully.

WANTED: SOUND ENGINEER

Job Description: Must be able to use headphones.

During the actual shoot you will be able to monitor most things. You will know if the actors flub a line. Cut! You will know when a prop falls over or when someone's cell phone rings. Cut! What you will not know is how well the actors' voices are being recorded on the tape or card. What you hear on set and what gets recorded on card are two totally different things, and it is quite possible that what sounds good to the whole crew may sound too soft or too loud on tape. Beyond

---

[2]If you don't get this joke, then ask your English teacher. She will think you are awesome for asking about literature outside of class. Reread Chapter 1 first, and be sure to throw in a Hawthorne reference when you talk to the teacher.

problems with volume, the microphone may be picking up things like the cough of a crew member, something that our brains filter out in everyday life. The cough will sound really ugly when it shows up in the final movie.

What you need to do, then, is assign one person to be in charge of audio for the whole shoot. Don't ask him to do anything else. Sound is that important. You wouldn't have your camera operator be in charge of anything else, and the same goes for your sound engineer. Pick someone whom you trust, hand him or her a job description, and promise a big fat credit at the end of the film. He or she will certainly deserve it.

Here is the sound engineer's actual description: Set up the sound equipment. Monitor the sound during shooting. Take down the sound equipment. It's that simple, but oh-so-important.

He must also be willing to stand his ground and stop the whole shoot. If he can hear a refrigerator humming, he must demand that it be unplugged. After all, he is accountable for this part of the production. If there is an air conditioning unit running just outside a window, turn the AC off. If a dog is barking outside or a plane flies overhead, time to re do the shot.

SHOTGUNS AND GRIPS

The biggest problem with sound in beginner films occurs when the crew uses the on-camera microphone to record audio. Since this mic is so far away from the action, the whole film feels far away. Suddenly the viewer finds herself outside of the movie rather than inside of it. The magic is gone.

In order to get close to the action, here is what you need: a shotgun mic, batteries (unless the camera supplies the mic with power through the XLR cable), a boom pole (preferably with a shock mount), cables, a grip to hold the boom pole, a grip to hold the cables, a sound engineer, and a camera that accepts XLR connections. If your camera does not accept XLR connections, then you will need to get a converter (Beachtek is a solid brand that mounts beneath the camera in the tripod screw hole). Another affordable option is to bypass the converter and buy the Audio Technica microphone mentioned in the gear chapter.

A shotgun mic is highly directional. Point it at a sound and it will primarily pick up that sound. Each mic is set to have a certain angle of pick up. Some are very narrow, and you have to be pointing right at the sound to hear it. Attach this mic to a pole and the boom operator's job is to point it at the sound you want to record.

Don't be afraid to get the boom pole really close to the faces of your actors. You will be amazed at how close you can get it and it still will not be seen in the shot. Often a team will practice beforehand, with the camera operator telling the boom op when the pole is in or out of the shot. Get as close as you can, but don't get in the shot.

As the boom pole operator follows the action with the mic and boom pole, she is very careful not to tap or touch the pole. It will sound really loud if she does. She can maneuver the pole by twisting it in the palm of her hand so that the mic points at one actor and then another. It's best to have the mic above the actors when possible, which makes this a tiring job that requires some arm strength. A grip walks behind her to keep her from tripping over the XLR cable that goes from the shotgun mic to the camera. This grip also makes sure that the audio cable does not get tight, thereby pulling over the camera, and that it never gets near an electrical wire. Extension cords can cause an unpleasant buzz in your audio. Cell phones can too, even if they are on silent. All cell phones must be off. Meanwhile, the sound engineer listens to the overall quality of the audio to make sure that it sounds good. Occasionally, he will talk to the boom operator to give some advice on what is working and what needs improving. On some sets, the sound engineer and the boom pole operator are one and the same. Ideally, both the sound engineer and the boom operator will be able to listen to the audio as it comes from the microphone. The easiest way to do this is to get a splitter that splits the headphones into two lines. Then run a long cord to the boom operator (tape it to the XLR cable). You can also use this technique to send an audio signal to the director.

Another way to hold a boom pole.

Here is how things will go down on the set: Once she confirms that the sound is working, the sound engineer lets the assistant director know that the sound team is ready to begin shooting. The assistant director is managing a lot of teams, so shooting may not begin right away. Be patient.

Before each shot, the assistant director will call, "Lock it up," and then, "Quiet on the set." Once it is quiet, the assistant director will ask, "Sound?" This is when the sound manager's job really begins. She must have a keen ear. Is the set quiet enough to begin shooting? Are there any extraneous noises that need to be shut down (like a computer hard drive or refrigerator)? All good? If yes, she says in a loud voice, "Ready" or "Speed."

Now the sound engineer is on, listening closely to everything through her head-phones. She must train herself to hear the things that our brain usually tunes out: the cough or a scuffling of feet or a slight hiss from an air conditioning vent that unexpectedly turned on. If a noise ruins a shot, she lets the assistant director know so that it can be shot again.

The sound engineer also monitors the sound level and quality of the actors' voices. If the mic accidentally shifts away from an actor's voice (too soft), the sound engineer needs to make the assistant director aware of it so the shot can be redone.

There is a chance that it will be easier to obtain a wireless lavaliere microphone instead of a shotgun microphone. With a lavaliere microphone, almost everything is the same as the boom pole setup except that the grips help to place the microphone onto the actor. They attach the transmitter to the microphone and a receiver to the camera. Of equal importance: They turn everything off when you are done. Leaving the mic on during the pizza break could kill your batteries and leave you in a bad way.

LOCATION WRAP, ALMOST
Everyone loves to hear "Location Wrap." Finally, we got the shot. Finally, we can go to the bathroom. Finally, we can....

"WAIT," says the sound engineer.

Before you leave the set you must, you absolutely must get some "natural sound" or "room tone." The sound engineer's job is to be pushy and make sure this happens without fail.

To get "room tone," have the assistant director call quiet on the set and then just record sound for two minutes. Make sure the actors and the props are in place. Now do it again, but this time have people moving or doing whatever they were doing during the scene except talking. Together, these sounds will become your number one tool in the editing studio. You will be way glad you did it.

Now it's a "Location Wrap." Not really.

Check the gate. Go back and replay a shot to make sure you got it and that it sounded good. Have the whole set be really quiet during playback. It is that important. The only danger here is that if you are using tape you could accidentally forget afterward to not fast-forward to the end of the shot. Next time you press record you might record over some great footage.

DO THE RIGHT THING

If you want to explore the depths of the human experience, sit in an editing room as the producer hears the words, "There is a hum in the audio," or worse yet, "We have no audio." The producer has two options: get everybody together again (not), or dub in the sound (never works). Leave dialogue replacement to the pros. Get audio right the first time. You will live a happier life.

RESHOOT

Sound ideas: Listen carefully.

▸ Sound is so important it deserves its own engineer.
▸ Avoid on-camera mics, use shotguns instead.
▸ Use headphones to monitor the quality of sound.
▸ Listen carefully for bad sounds (hums, buzzes, snuffles and shuffles).
▸ Get "room tone" before wrapping a location.

CHAPTER 11

EDITING

READY

Add up all the time that you've put into this project as well as all the time that each crew member has put into the project. The number of hours devoted to your production will be in the hundreds, at least. Think about it. Hundreds of hours and it all ends up on just a handful of tapes or cards or hard drive. It makes sense to treat your media with a little respect.

Clearly label the tapes and their cases. Keep them off of the dashboard and out of your back pocket. Avoid speakers since they have magnets in them which could ruin the tapes, and don't leave the tapes on the breakfast table (got milk?). Most important of all, slide the little "no record" button on the tape. Forget this one and you will be voted off of the island. .

If you are shooting on cards and then storing your footage on hard drive, spend the extra money and get a second back-up hard drive. It will be the best money you spend.

Get the taped footage onto a hard drive as soon as you can. We will tell you how a little later in this chapter. Then put the tapes in a super safe place as a back-up in case the hard drive crashes or a file gets deleted.

AIM

Check out Chapter 12 for info about film festivals. Pick one and use its submission deadline as your editing deadline. Be strong and make no compromises. Remember the main rule of this book: You must finish your film.

EDIT

Some of the best times of your filmmaking career will be spent in the editing studio. It's a dark and magical place where you breathe life into your work. Fictional characters come alive, known only to you. Nights turn into days turn into nights. You enter dreamtime. Daily life becomes irrelevant as you get lost in your art.

THE EDITING STUDIO

For many first-time moviemakers, their editing studio is simply their computer desk. If you can, though, try to go a step further and make a little studio.

We encourage students to find a basement or unused bedroom in which to set up. A dedicated workspace allows you to be more serious. Without extra distractions, you can concentrate on the movie. Plus, it becomes like a little clubhouse. Make it dark. Get a few extra chairs so that you can test your work on friends and family.

Carve out a large enough space where you can lay out your screenplay or take notes on what scenes you do and don't like. You will also need room for your computer, your camera, a television, and a good pair of speakers.

Here is the setup. Since your camera is digital, it has a little four-pin FireWire port into which you plug the FireWire cable that came with your camera. This cable also connects to the six-pin FireWire port on your computer. FireWire ports are standard issue on Apple computers, and for about twenty bucks you can buy a FireWire card for your PC. These cards are often called by their technical name: IEEE 1394.

Your camera talks to the computer over this FireWire, sending the information off of your cards or tapes. It also receives images from the computer, and this is how you will record your final movie back onto tape if required.

Since the computer sends images to your camera, you can redirect these images to a television and watch the movie as you edit without all of the computer software interface showing. This is the same setup that you used for a monitor during production. For most cameras this means connecting the yellow RCA out to the yellow RCA in on the television. The camera needs to be in VCR mode instead of record mode, and you won't need to be recording while you are watching the edit.

Your TV also allows you to watch your movie on a bigger screen. This helps you to keep an eye on how well the video is focused as well as other little details (like a microphone) that might get missed on a little computer screen, although sometimes TVs overscan and don't show you the whole image.

Next, remember the importance of getting good sound? When your movie is shown before big crowds, the speakers are going to be darn good. If all you do is edit on your computer's little puny speaker(s), you won't hear everything that got recorded to tape. You will get to your premiere and sounds will jump out at you that you never heard before, like a crew member, or the wind, or an airplane.

To avoid this surprise, use the audio out function of your camera to send your sound (using the red and white RCA outputs) to a television or, better yet, to a stereo receiver that is connected to some kickin' speakers. Turn it up loud and physically separate the right and left speakers. Now you will be simulating what will happen when you show it in a nice theater. You will edit with confidence knowing that the person on the left side of the screen won't be speaking through the right speaker while the left speaker picks up the sneeze of a crew member.

THE COMPUTER

Video editing programs can really push a computer to its limits. Whereas you can write a paper using the chip inside your wristwatch, you can't video edit on it. The speed of your computer as well as the amount of memory it has can make a big difference while editing. A big hard drive comes in handy, too, since video takes up a lot of disk space.

Chances are that you will be using a computer that you already own. While you cannot do a lot about its speed, you can add RAM for dirt-cheap. It's really easy to install, so if you cannot do it, find someone who can (i.e. the technology consultant for your movie).

In terms of hard drive space, the amount you need will vary depending on what format you shoot in. In 1080P, a minute of footage can take one GB of hard drive space, although this will vary depending on what type of compression your camera does internally. Not only do you need space for all of your shots, but also the final version of the movie. Then if you make it into a DVD, you will need at a minimum of five more gigs. Purchasing an external dedicated hard drive is a great idea. You can get them cheaply at an electronics superstore similar to Fry's Electronics.

MAC vs. PC

Amazingly enough, there are still a lot of people who argue about which is better: a Mac or a PC. Maybe it is because authors like us use the word "versus" as if it is a battle. The answer to this false dilemma is to use what you've got.

At the same time, we are a little biased toward Apple for one reason: Apple develops both the software that runs its computers as well as the computer themselves. In addition, Apple develops its own movie-making and DVD-making software. As a result, they are able to coordinate the whole system so that it works smoothly.

THE SOFTWARE

Just like with computers, don't worry a lot about what program you use to edit. All programs are pretty similar, and once you know one, you can learn another one in just a few hours. Work hard at getting a professional-level package such as Apple's Final Cut Pro or Adobe Premiere. The entry-level packages do work, but it's harder to get them to do the some of the things that we are going to recommend later in this chapter.

Pro software packages can be a little pricey, so before you buy one you might look to the maker's website to see if a trial version is offered. Check and see if your school has a package available. We recommend that you look to Apple's Final Cut Express, a scaled down version of Final Cut Pro that students can buy for really cheap.

Don't freak out if you cannot get the software you want. We recently attended a student film festival in which one of the best entries was cut on iMovie, Apple's free entry-level software that comes with new Macs. It has been really improved each year, so if you do not have the latest version it may make sense to buy it. Again, check for the substantial student discount.

The rest of this chapter is written from the Final Cut perspective, so if you are using other software you may have to translate a little. In the end, though, all the concepts are the same. A fade-to-black is still a fade-to-black, no matter what corporation you are feeding.

DOWNLOADING YOUR FOOTAGE

Recording to cards makes downloading footage really easy. You just transfer them to a hard drive like a file transfer. Once you use this technique you will never want to use tape again. Before you start editing, organize your footage into folders corresponding to each scene. Your bedroom can be messy, but here you need to be organized since you might be pulling from each take as you cut back and forth in a complicated scene.

Check your tape to make sure the "no record" switch is engaged. Then stick it in the camera and put the camera in VCR mode. Start up your editing software and then put your software in capture mode (as opposed to editing mode). Press play on the camera, and as you see the footage you want to capture, click on the "start capture" button. You can actually press play from the computer program, if you prefer. Once you are done, press the escape button. If you want to, you can capture multiple takes all at once and then just divide them up once they are on the computer, or you can capture one take at a time.

A more efficient way to get your video onto hard drive is to watch the video and find the timecodes of where you want to start and stop capturing footage. You can then tell the computer these two numbers, and it will do the work for you. There will be no guessing as to when to press the start and stop capturing buttons. Some software allows you to enter a bunch of these numbers and then tell the computer to go to work while you go see a movie. When you come back, all the scenes are conveniently loaded onto the hard drive.

THE CONCEPT OF EDITING — NONLINEAR AND
NON-DESTRUCTIVE EDITING

Back in our day we edited barefoot in the snow on a videotape machine that was powered by firewood which we had cut with our bare hands while we snacked on raw beets.

You've heard it before. A bunch of old farts telling you how easy it is for you and how hard it was for them. But it is true; things were different back in our day. We did not edit on computers. Instead, we had to rewind and fast forward to the precise points we liked and then press record on a second machine.

Now that digital filmmaking has arrived, you have arrived. This book and your ability to make great films as a teenager would not exist if it were not for digital video. So it might be worth peeking behind the curtain to see what digital video editing does for you.

NONLINEAR

Your algebra teacher may or may not love this one.

Remember linear equations from algebra class? They were straight lines: $y=mx+b$. So what does nonlinear mean? In math class it means curved lines. That's just in math class. Here it means you can work on things out of sequence. You don't have to work on scene one first and then scene two and then scene three. Instead, you can jump ahead to scene four or even the middle of scene four and work on it first.

You probably take tests in a nonlinear way. If you can do problem five, that is where you start. How ironic is it that you take linear equations tests using nonlinear methods? Do you think your math teacher understands irony? Are you using irony in your short? Do you like Alanis Morissette? There is a movie with Alanis Morissette called *Dogma*. There is a group of filmmakers called Dogme.

NON-DESTRUCTIVE

Once your raw footage has been captured onto a computer, you will never touch it again. We don't mean the tapes, although hopefully you will never need to touch them again, either. Instead, what we mean is that the video file on your computer will never be changed. You will just point to it and read from it.

The software that edits your movie does not actually save video each time you save the movie. Instead, it saves a list of instructions that point to the movie files saved on your hard drive. Luckily you don't have to understand these instructions; all you do is point and click.

Let's say that you started the camera rolling, but the scene really does not begin until the third second of tape. Then at the eleventh second your take ended. When using actual film, cutting actually means cutting. You would go to the third second and cut the film for the beginning of your shot. Then you would go to the eleventh second and cut the film for the end of your shot.

With digital video, cutting means pointing. The computer is thinking, "Find the file on the computer that corresponds to this scene. Then find three seconds into that scene. Show the footage starting here and then stopping at the eleventh second." The clip that it shows you is just an unmodified portion of the original segment. If it turns out that the clip is too short, all you do is drag it a little longer and the computer will change "eleven" to "eleven AND A HALF" seconds. With film you would have been out of luck because you would have already cut it.

When all is said and done with your movie, you will export a completely new video file that takes all the original files and puts them together according to the instructions you give it. Again, the original files are left unchanged. This new video file is your actual movie, and you could still make a completely new and different movie out of the old footage.

THE DOWNSIDE: EDITING ZOMBIES

Digital video allows you to test and play with your footage over and over again. Be careful, though, since this leads to a medical condition called editus infinitus. Catch this disease and you may never finish your short.

Secondly, there is an art to editing. Too often we see students just throw down clips to see how they work. This disease is called editus experimentalis. It is a weird disease because it can sometimes lead to some cool results. But more often than not, it leads to a limited work that has yet to meet its potential. Re-stated, it looks like the filmmaker did not know some basic things about editing that would have really helped his or her short.

Instead of just throwing down some scenes, practice the craft of editing. Don't get us wrong. A little or a lot of experimentation is great, but do it intelligently. Know what you are experimenting with. Know that a dissolve is more common than a wipe. Know how a wipe works. Once you do, it is ok to play with a wipe because you know that it might not work.

THE CRAFT

Most stories are not told in real time. If they were, movies would not only be boring, but they would also take a lifetime to watch. Instead, movies jump around through time. While the overall structure of where a movie goes in time is determined by the script, the editor still has a lot of creative control over the mechanics of the jumping. He may decide where exactly is the best spot to jump to the next scene. He may also decide what kind of transition occurs.

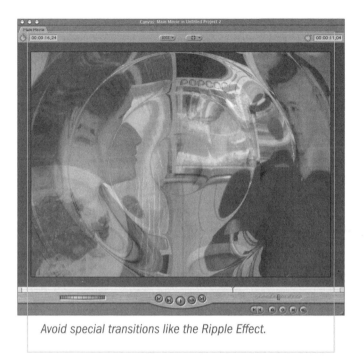

Avoid special transitions like the Ripple Effect.

Digital video is pretty amazing because it makes transitional effects easy, almost too easy. For example, when you change from one scene to the next, you can choose a ripple effect, a clock wipe, a star iris, an explode, or a three-banded slide. And if you do, you will be labeled as a beginning video editor who is slap-happy with all the effects in his new program.

Unless you have a really good reason to get funky with your transitions, we recommend that you stick with cuts, dissolves, and fades. Exceptions might be a dream sequence, a Star Wars parody, a comedy, or when you just break the rules. In the end we like to play it safe by sticking to transitions that don't draw attention to themselves.

CUTS

A cut is the simplest of all transitions. One shot ends and the next one begins. But don't be fooled by its simplicity. There is still a lot to think about. For example, are the two shots similar or different in terms of framing, pacing, color, or action?

Are they so different as to be shocking? Maybe you want the transition to be shocking. If the shots are similar, are they so similar that the viewer won't realize that things have changed?

If you are telling a story in real time, pay close attention to movement and continuity. Make sure that the action in one shot flows into the next. See if the clouds have changed or the angle at which an actor is sitting has changed. Little discrepancies add up, and your viewer will detect that something is wrong even if she cannot tell you what it is.

Be careful never to go backwards in time. For example, if someone is walking toward a door and her left foot is about to hit the ground, don't cut to a different shot that has her left foot higher off of the ground. It will look like a glitch in the Matrix. In contrast, there are times when you can fast forward by a fraction of a second and no one will notice.

Pay attention to where your eye is drawn from one shot to the next. Our eyes tend to follow action and faces. If your cut requires the viewer's eyes to dart from the lower left one frame to the upper right in the next, this can be jarring. The viewer might also miss something.

DISSOLVES

Dissolves signify a gradual transition. Often they indicate that a change is taking place, either through time in the same scene or into a totally different scene. The length of a dissolve significantly affects how the transition is perceived, so be sure to experiment with length.

Dissolves require that there be enough footage from both scenes to cover the dissolve. Beginning editors get frustrated when they put two shots together and then try to make a dissolve. The computer won't let them and they don't know why. The reason is that the end of one shot is touching the beginning of the next shot. They need to overlap to get the dissolve, or any effect for that matter.

Another problem occurs when the dissolve lasts for too long. As you dissolve out of one shot, you get to a point in the footage where the director has yelled cut. Maybe the actor moves his hand or he starts to sit down. Even if this happens for only 1/30 of a second, people will still notice it.

FADES

Fades signify major beginning and endings. Fading to black signifies a major transition. Since there is nothing to look at but color, the audience gets a moment to reflect. Be careful not to overuse fades. Save them for when you really need them.

BE PRECISE

After you have a rough cut of a particular scene, go over it again with an eye for detail. Use the arrow keys to move back and forth through each transition frame by frame. Things will pop out at you that you don't see when the movie is playing at full speed.

You might ask: "If they didn't pop out at me the first time, then why should I care?" The answer is that someone else might see them. As you repeatedly watch your movie, you will get used to putting your eye on the same spot each time you watch it. By stop framing, you can look at each frame and explore what other viewers might be seeing.

Sometimes cutting off a third of a second can make a world of a difference in an edit.

TELLING THE STORY

Since you only have five minutes to tell your story, you don't have the luxury of exploring the location where a scene is taking place. Instead, you need to make quick suggestions.

An establishing shot lets the viewer know where the actors are, and it often in-cludes some common objects that quickly help the viewers figure out what they are seeing. Humans can get a lot of information out of a two-second shot. In fact, music videos and commercials contain shots that last less than a second.

Let's say you are jumping from a high school couple on a Friday night date to Monday's lunch table. In between the two shots, you might want to insert a quick outside view of the school that includes a school bus. The viewer will then know that the movie has returned to school. If you did not have the establishing shot, someone unfamiliar with the school might think that the picture of the dude eating spaghetti is the same restaurant scene but at a different angle. Yes, you can laugh at the idea of someone confusing your cafeteria with a restaurant, but it could happen, especially if your shots are tight and the dialogue is quick.

When the scene motivates you to do so, cut to other shots. As an editor, it is too easy to let one shot tell the whole story. Instead, make sure that you have some cuts. Let's return to the Monday lunch table. Your main actor is eating and thinking about Friday night when his phone rings. His head jerks to look at the phone. He picks it up and answers it.

Instead of letting one take roll in which you get everything, go back to your footage and look for the best close-up shot of him picking up the phone. You may even have forgotten that you have the shot, so spend some time reviewing your footage.

Don't let the actor finish his head jerk. Instead, cut on the action and go right to the close-up of the phone. This is also an example of where you can jump forward in time. As you cut to the close-up, his hand could already be reaching for the phone even though it might be physically impossible for him to have his hand there yet. If you are worried about this, play with it until it works for you, and then test it on another viewer.

A big mistake that we see in student films is when an editor cuts to the close up of the hand with the hand still, and then one fourth of a second later the hand starts to move to the phone. Trim off that one quarter-second of stopped hand.

BE CRUEL, BE KIND

A good short film should sweep you up, plunge you into its world, and then spit you out before you can ever realize that any time has passed. Most short films, however, seem to last longer than they really are. We have yet to meet a physicist who can explain to us how five minutes can seem like twenty when watching a boring film. But it happens.

We may not be able to explain how it happens, but here is why it happens. First, filmmakers get emotionally attached to their footage. They end up keeping a beautiful shot or one with a friend in it when they should have cut it out. Unless a shot pushes your movie forward, it must be cut. We can forgive you for being attached to it, but you must be cruel to be kind. If it does not hurt to cut something, then it should already have been cut. If it does hurt to cut something, then you are on the path to making your work a short.

Another reason for shorts being too long is plain old sloppy editing. The editor will throw down a rough cut and then just leave it at that. It looks pretty good — to the editor. And of course it looks good, relatively speaking. He just took a jumbled mess of shots and made it into a story. The story now needs polishing, though.

Just like with an English paper, you have to revise your work. Each shot and each transition needs to be examined. Trim a half-second here or a quarter-second there. Ask yourself why you chose certain takes over others. We have seen far too many student films that would have been awesome with just one more pass.

Recall the establishing shot at the school with a school bus. A common mistake would be to linger on the school bus four seconds when the audience probably got the point within the first second. For the next three seconds your audience starts to slip out of your fiction. The movie gets long.

Remember that your film is a short film. Tell your story and get out. Please. We have seen too many long short films. They feel like this paragraph. They never seem to end. Just like this paragraph never seems to end. They just go on and on. When will it end? They keep telling the story, the story about the paragraph that never ends. And as they tell their story that never ends, the viewer has mentally tuned out.

Restated: This is a short film. Tell your story and get out.

SOUND

In Chapter 9 we advised that half of your film is in the audio. As you edit, make sure that you are monitoring your audio on a decent set of speakers like we described at the beginning of this chapter.

All rooms have a certain sound to them. You don't typically notice it, but even right now if you stop for a moment, there are things that your ear will pick up. Microphones hear the same things, only better. Even within the same room, the sound can change as the microphone changes its direction.

As you put your scenes together, changes in background sound can become very noticeable, especially on the speakers where you show your movie. So get a good pair of speakers and play it loud.

Check out the timeline below. When the guy reaches for his telephone, the background sound changes. As a result, the audience will notice. They will suddenly realize they are watching a movie.

One way to solve this problem is to unlink the audio and the video and then drag his audio to the end of the cell phone cutaway. The audience expects the background sound to be the same, so they will never notice your trickery.

Another way to tackle this issue is to put in some separate background noise. Even though the cafeteria scene happens on a Monday, you might have shot it on a Saturday when there were no people in the room. To make the scene look like it was filmed on a Monday, put in a totally new audio track that has cafeteria noise in it.

Viewers will hear the sound change.

What if you wanted to do a voice over of this guy's thoughts as he eats his lunch? If the voice over is recorded in a different room, it will sound different than the cafeteria, and the difference will be painfully obvious. Of course, the loud cafeteria noise ("walla") will cover some of the difference.

Sounddogs.com is a great place to get specialized sound effects.

AUDIO FADES

Whenever a sound changes, it is a really good idea to have the sound fade out really quickly rather than just having it cut off. Due to the way speakers work and the way we hear things, when audio just stops, we notice. Often it sounds like a little "pop." If it fades away, we are less likely to notice it ending. A cross dissolve is also very appropriate as one sound changes into another. Experiment with having a fade on all audio. It can be as short as four frames, with eight frames being a nice compromise. The length largely depends on the shot and what you think sounds good.

AUDIO AS TRANSITION

Start paying attention to transitions in movies. Sometimes you will hear the next scene before it shows up on the screen, and other times the sound from one scene will run into the next, even after the video is gone. These transitions provide a subliminal smoothness to your sound.

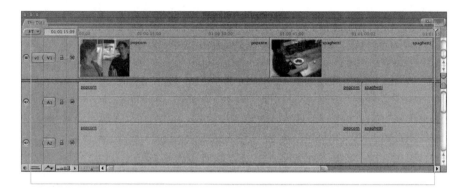

SOUNDTRACKS

Music greatly affects the mood of a movie, especially if you are using a hip song that people really identify with. The problem is that most of the music that you have in your collection is copyrighted. This means someone owns it and that you have to ask his or her permission to use it.

A lot of our students begin to learn filmmaking by editing with other people's music. It's a useful exercise since they know the songs well. They get better at achieving the video mood if they know the audio mood.

As long as a video is not going beyond your home television set, then you probably won't get in trouble for using someone else's music.

But there is an even bigger reason for not using someone else's music: Your film might show in festivals or make it onto television. The last thing you want is to make it big and then have to re-edit your whole film to a new song. It might completely change your film.

If you are using a movie as part of your portfolio to get into college or as a calling card for a summer job, people in positions of power will notice that you steered clear of doing what every other movie-making kid in the nation is already doing. You will be different. People who work in the business will respect you for keeping it legal.

Most of all, it's your movie. And if you use someone else's music, your movie will be good not because you made it good, but because of the music you put in it. Make it your own.

If you must use copyrighted music, getting permission is not impossible. You have to write the publisher and the musician, and you will probably have to pay some money. The amount of money you spend is less when you only buy the "festival rights" for the song. Local bands are a lot more cool about this thing than international mega-bands, but in the end, though, all of this work is usually more hassle than it is worth. If you are determined to go this route, check out *http://www.copyrightkids.org* for further help.

Programs like Apple's Garage Band allow you to program your own music with riffs like seventies funk or classical pieces. There are musicians on the Internet who give away their music for free as long as you give them credit.

Alternately, try to get a school orchestra to play a classical piece that has no copyright. Do you have a friend that plays piano or violin? Also, local, unsigned bands might be really excited to give you some of their music. Optimally, get a friend to score the movie with an original soundtrack. Maybe let him or her know what other artists you think fit, and he or she can imitate their style.

One other thing about music: Don't let the length of a song dictate the length of your movie. You will start using video as filler to get to the end of the song.

FINAL SOUNDTRACK
Once you have edited your whole movie, turn up the sound and leave it at the same level for the duration of your short. Don't make the mistake of adjusting the stereo or TV volume since you will lose track of how loud each segment is in relationship to other ones.

Next play the whole movie, listening for anything that is too loud or soft.

Watch your program's audio meters, being sure to not let the average audio level go above -6dB. This won't seem right at first, but when you ship your video off to the Discovery Channel, it is what they will want.

PUTTING IT IN THE CAN
Find some people who know nothing about your film and ask them to watch it. Some fresh eyes will be very helpful in catching anything that you might have missed.

Then, once you are satisfied with your movie, export it to the hard drive as a self-contained movie. This is different than simply saving it. When you save your movie, you are just saving the instructions the computer uses to put the movie together. When you export it, you get a whole new movie.

As you export it, don't resize it or mathematically encode it (called a codec). These codecs are great for Internet delivery, but they take the quality of the movie way down.

Once you have this full resolution copy, go ahead and export a smaller version for digital distribution (see Chapter 13). While your editor should have an export feature, these are often difficult to understand and of lower quality. Instead, try QuickTimePro (Mac and PC). It is relatively cheap and does a lot of things for you like saving movies from the web. Most of all it makes exporting easy. It has a feature called "Export for Web" which is fairly accessible. It also has a full-fledged export function. A five-minute movie exported from QuickTimePro at 640x360 pixels using the h.264 codec at medium quality should get you under 100 Mb. Also be sure to check the box "Prepare for Internet Streaming" since this will allow it to play faster from your own website if you create one. Maximum allowed file sizes and codecs change frequently, so check out the requirements on You-Tube, since it sets the Internet upload standard.

You should also copy your completed short onto mini-DV tape for safekeeping or onto multiple hard drives. You could also burn the final exported movie as data onto a DVD disc. This is different than making a DVD that will play on televisions. Of course you can also make a DVD that does play on televisions. Apple's iDVD is easy-to-use software that comes free with Macintoshes that have DVD burners.

RESHOOT
Editing: The cutting room floor.

- ▸ Take care of your tapes.
- ▸ Use monitor and speakers as you edit.
- ▸ Large external drive and a fast processor matter more than brand or software.
- ▸ Non-destructive digital editing is great, but can be endless. Deadlines!
- ▸ Stick with cuts, dissolves, and fades as transitions.
- ▸ Cut ruthlessly. Keep the film moving forward.
- ▸ Listen carefully as you edit; sound can be a transition element, too.
- ▸ Get permission for copyrighted music, or find alternatives.

CHAPTER

12

GETTING
NOTICED

WOW! YOU'VE FINISHED

Welcome to the club. That one percent that got their butts off the couch and actually made a movie. Whisper to yourself, "I am a filmmaker."

Look, we are not just stroking your ego. We have seen lots of students (and adults for that matter) try to make a film and fail. Some never get past the script, others shoot only a few scenes, while others are to this day living in a permanent state of editing. But you did it. You really do deserve kudos.

Now, what are you going to do with your short?

ONE FESTIVAL, FOR NOW

In Chapter 11 we encouraged you to find one film festival and use its entry date as your own deadline. Now is the time to send your baby off into the big world of film festivals.

The process of applying to festivals can be a little daunting. It requires paperwork, and some festivals want to see any press you may have gotten. There might even be an entry fee. Don't stress out. Just get the movie onto tape or DVD, fill out their application as best you can, and send it in. If you don't have any press clippings, don't worry. If your cast and crew list is a little rough, don't worry. You will get it all in order by the time you get to the second festival entry. For now, though, just send your film in.

Nikos Theodosakis keeps a great list of festivals at his website: *http://www.thedirectorintheclassroom.com/festivals4.php*

THEN GO LOCAL

When thinking about what to do with your film, the sky is the limit. You may make it into Sundance or onto HBO. But first we want you to think locally.

Show your movie at a school or a local theater. Not only do you owe it to your crew, you owe it to yourself. Nothing is better than seeing your film on the big screen. Okay, one thing is better: the applause after the showing.

The cautious side of you may be wondering: "Who will come?" or, "Will people like it?" Read on.

Go to your credits and count the number of people who participated or assisted with your film. Now list all the people who kind of helped out but didn't get a credit, like the guy who gave you permission to shoot in his dumpster or the woman who lent you the Gucci handbag. Now list all of the people who have heard about the film, like your family, your friends and their friends. Boom. You have an audience. More importantly, you have a receptive audience.

If you want even more people to come, team up with other young filmmakers and host your own youth film festival. We really like this idea since it makes for a full evening. Your audience will enjoy the variety as well.

LOCATION

First, find a place to show it. Your school's theater or auditorium is the best bet because everyone knows where it is, and it is free. All you need is your film, a screen and a projector. Add some popcorn for good taste.

You aren't limited to your school. Another option is to rent a movie theater or playhouse. Independent movie theaters will probably be more receptive than big chains. Playhouses are great because they are cozy and usually in need of a little dough. Either way, ask if a daytime slot is cheaper than an evening one, although we are partial to the Thursday or Friday night slot.

Sometimes you might have no other choice than to look beyond school. The language or content in your short might put you into the PG-13 or R category. Do the math and you can see why your teacher or principal may have to say no. Be respectful of their predicament as well as larger cultural issues at stake. Watch Bowling for Columbine.

If you have the choice between a smaller theater (100 seats) and a larger theater (up to 500 seats), go for the smaller theater. A packed theater feels better.

A small independent theater.

BIG, DARK AND LOUD: AV

With luck, someone at your school can score you a projector, not the classic reel-to-reel kind, but an LCD projector. If you can get more pixels or more brightness, do so, because this usually means other features (like color) are better too.

If you strike out at school, then start asking adults what they wear to work. Suits use LCD projectors more than they use coffeemakers, and they don't use either on Friday nights when they are not at work.

If you are at an independent movie theater, chances are that it already has an LCD projector for you to use, but you may be charged an extra fee for the set up and for an employee to be there.

Finally, you can easily rent an LCD projector. Look under audio-visual in the phone book.

THE HOOK UP

Dump your film to tape or burn it onto a DVD. Then connect an RCA cable from your camera's or your DVD player's yellow RCA output to the LCD projector's input.

Some LCD projectors also have an S-Video input, which makes for a slightly better picture than an RCA cable. You could also show your short right from your computer's hard drive by using the monitor-in slot on the projector.

As for your audio, be prepared to crank it up. Remember, the audience is listening. See if you can get someone in the theater department to help hook up your camera or DVD player to the main audio system. This usually entails taking the red and white RCA outputs from your camera or DVD player and then and converting them to XLR. If you are using a computer-to-projector setup, you will need to convert the audio out on your computer (usually a 1/8 plug) to XLR. Sometimes when you convert to XLR you get a buzzing sound. Go to Radio Shack and ask for a little device that will help you "impedance match" the system audio to your audio. Always do a sound check before the big night.

If you cannot hook into the theater's main audio, then bring your own receiver and speakers from home. Your receiver has RCA inputs.

PROMOTION

Once you have a location, date and time, think about a little promotion before the big show. Promotion is actually pretty fun and will help you create a handy press kit when you start shopping your work.

POSTERS AND POSTCARDS

Find a few of your favorite movie posters on the Internet and decide what you like about them. Pay attention to color schemes, text placement, number of images, and types of images. Use what you learn along with your high-resolution production stills to make a promotional 11 x 17 poster. Since by now you are way experienced in getting people to help you, look to a studio art student for some help.

If you forgot to take production stills, then restage a shot. You can also export a still image from your movie, but you will need to de-interlace it either in the movie-editing program or in Photoshop.

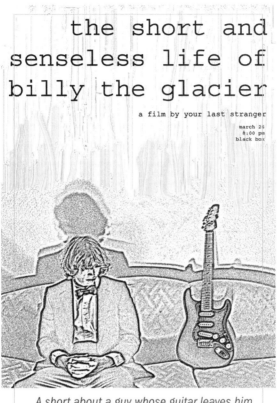

A short about a guy whose guitar leaves him and the struggles he endures to find her.

You can use most any image-editing software to make these, but we really like Adobe Photoshop, Adobe Illustrator, or Adobe Elements. Of the three, Adobe Elements is the easiest to use and the cheapest to buy. Chances are that your yearbook staff or someone in the art department will have one of these software packages. If you cannot find a copy, trial versions are available at *www.adobe.com*.

Whatever program you are using, set your document resolution at 300 dots per inch (dpi) so that the poster doesn't look pixilated when you print it. Vertical movie posters are more common than horizontal posters. Avoid cutesy fonts. Use simple yet stylish images and make your title dominant.

In addition to the title of your movie, include the date, time, location, and cost (we suggest free), as well as a website if you have one. Be careful to design your poster so that it still looks cool if you delete these items. You will need a dateless poster for publicity later on.

Now save the poster in three different sizes: 11 x 17, 8.5 x 11, and 4 x 6. The 11 x 17 and 8.5 x 11 versions can be used as posters. Send the 8.5 x 11 and the 4 x 6 along with festival entries. The 4 x 6 card also makes for a great handout as people get off the bus or as a personal invitation to the premier. Send the 4 x 6 by mail to your actors, crew, and financiers. Somehow mailing the card makes it feel like a present to them. Not only will they be thrilled to get it, it is a great way to say thank you. Chances are they will save it as a memento of the production.

While the 11 x 17 may be too large to print at home, most everything else you can print fairly well using a desktop printer. You can also take your work on a CD to FedEx Office (fast but pricey) or a professional printer (requires planning but cheaper). Think about getting posters printed in color, but stick with black and white if you are running low on cash. For the 4 x 6 postcards, look to an office supply store that sells precut sheets to go in your own printer. Also look for printers on the Internet. You can send your document electronically and have them print anything we have mentioned here fairly cheaply.

Finally, treat yourself to a poster that is bigger than 11 x 17. You and your bedroom walls deserve it.

TICKETS

Print tickets for the big event. Office supply stores sell sheets of blank business cards that are just the right size for a ticket, and the cards often come with a Word template to use in the design process. If you can, integrate the image from your poster onto the ticket.

These tickets are not the kind you sell at the door. In fact, we don't recommend you sell tickets for the event at all. Instead, think of these tickets as promotional tool. Use them to invite people to the opening. If people have a ticket, they feel special and are more likely to come. They also now have a physical reminder of the time, date and location.

If you are short on cash, or just want to repay your loans, put a donations jar at the door, and make an announcement about it before the movie starts.

Try this publicity stunt. Make the tickets a hot item. While anyone can come to the film, only people with tickets are guaranteed entry and a seat. For example, from 7:30 until 7:50, allow ticketed patrons to enter the theater. Then anyone without a ticket can fill up the remaining seats from 7:50 until 8:00. A great thing about this plan is that it gets everyone there on time. If you try this method, explain it clearly on the tickets and on the poster.

Give each filmmaker in your festival ten tickets, and only ten tickets, to give away. If you are just showing one film, then give each actor ten tickets. During school announcements, give away a few tickets to people who can correctly identify a line from a movie. Set a day and time when students can come to the drama department and pick up tickets.

The trick is to make tickets seem scarce, which will make people want them even more. If you have picked a small theater then they might actually be scarce. If you are in a big theater, let the unlucky ticketless ones know that they will still get in as long as they get there right at 7:50 when you give away the remaining seats. Of course, this is stretching the truth a little bit because you might sell out. Welcome this problem with open arms.

WEBSITE

Create a website for your production. If you really want to go pro, register a domain name that includes the title of your movie. Like your script, a website shows that you are serious, plus it is a quick and cheap way to show people your work. Put a copy of your poster and maybe even a short trailer. If the website comes with an email address, then you can use this for festival applications.

Better yet, develop a website for your new production company. Its main feature will be your short — and then your next short, and then the next one. This website will become both a portfolio and an evolving work of art.

Another option is to use YouTube as your website (see Chapter 13).

PRESS

Getting an article written about your production or festival will help to bring people to the show. There are two additional reasons to get some press.

First, it helps you with festival entries.

Next, it may give you exposure to people in the biz. You never know, maybe a movie executive lives just down the street and will read about you in the monthly neighborhood update.

Stick with it and try to get at least one bit of press, no matter how small.

Your school newspaper might want to do a story on your show. If not, then write one for them. A city-wide newspaper might be interested, especially if you have teamed up with other young filmmakers to put on a festival. Look to your town's weekly arts paper. Think also about a lower-scale, community newsletter. Or think larger scale and hit the television stations.

In order to get press, you need to develop a press release. Below is a sample press release for you to use. Fax and email it to any news outlet you want. Maybe even follow up with a phone call. Find the person in charge of local news or entertainment, and make sure to contact him or her personally. Look in the phone book, on web pages, or in the publication itself for contact information.

Be careful with what you put on the press release. Depending on what you and your parents think is appropriate, you may not want to list the place and time that you will show your film. A journalist is not likely to crash your party, but some weirdo from the general public might. Do be sure to include a phone number at the bottom of the press release because the news outlet might need to contact you. As long as it is not part of the text of the press release proper, this phone number should not get printed. Regardless, consider using your parents' number or a teacher's work number rather than your cell number.

Production Company Name
2900 Bunny Run Road, Austin Texas, 78746

Put the address of your webpage or YouTube page here
Phone – 512-555-1212
Fax – 512-555-1212

Insert email address here
PRESS RELEASE
FOR IMMEDIATE RELEASE
Contact: Jane Spartan
Phone: 512-555-1212

Austin High School Student Produces Her Own Film

Austin, TX, September 25, 2010 — Jane Spartan, a high school student at Spartan High School, has produced and directed her own film using an all-high school cast and crew.

The film, "Bicycles in Love," tells the story of two bikes that decide to ditch their owners and run away together.

Since she was five years old, Jane Spartan has wanted to make films. At age nine, she was staging mock films on the playground. Then, at the age of thirteen, she got her own camera. By fifteen she had written, produced, and edited her own film.

What makes Jane's movie different from the average teen skateboard video is that she actually turned the process into a real movie production. She held auditions. She recruited friends to help with sound and lighting. Most importantly, she learned real movie-making lessons like how to keep her crew fed.

Jane will be showing her film locally as part of the *Insert your film festival name here* film festival in February.

Page Two

Jane has already submitted her film to a national film festival, and will soon be vying for a slot on the international film festival circuit.

"Bicycles in Love" has led this young filmmaker to start her own production company called Spartan Studios.

Keep your eyes on this young Spielberg. We can all say we knew her when.

***

For further information, contact Jack Spartanhead at 512-555-1212

THE BIG NIGHT

Feel the buzz. People are strolling in, wanting to say hi to you. There is a gentle murmur in the theater. Some cool tunes are playing. You are a little nervous but relaxed enough to schmooze and say some thank yous.

Here is why you are relaxed: First, you finished editing a long time ago. Do not do any last-minute edits. Invariably you will lose the file, crash your computer, or change your movie for the worst. Stick by your original work.

Next, you got to the theater a few hours early and tested everything. Technology will go bad when you most need it, so prepare ahead of time. Better yet, test it a day in advance.

Finally, the big relaxer. You have a few friends helping you with the showing. Let them turn on the projector, the DVD player, and the sound.

Your job is to be the filmmaker, not the film presenter.

WHAT TO SAY

Remember how during shooting your tone affected the attitude of the whole crew. Well, the same goes for your premiere. Before the film starts, formally welcome everyone in the audience. Let them know how much you appreciate them coming. Recognize some key people in the audience by having them stand up (don't overdo this; save it for the person who funded something or worked on the project well beyond expectations). Next, thank your whole cast and crew.

If you are sponsoring a mini-festival, think about having a panel discussion afterwards. Get all the student producers in front of the audience and have them answer questions. Your tone is important here as well. If you want serious questions, you will need to behave seriously.

Tell the crowd that you are interested in their opinions. Ask them to email you and tell you what worked and what didn't work. This feedback is really important for you as a growing filmmaker.

Finally, have mom or dad take some pictures at the premiere. You will want to remember it, and E! will want the pictures when they do a background story on you.

FESTIVALS

Don't start with Sundance. Get your feet wet first (that is, unless Sundance's deadline is about to happen, in which case you should go for it). Start small and look locally. While film festivals are national and international in scope, youth film festivals often focus on local productions first. You have the best chance on your home turf, and this local success will help you get into other, bigger festivals. Buzz generates buzz.

Look for festivals that specifically have a teen or high school section. Don't get confused by the term student film. Some festivals take this to mean college student films.

Also, don't waste your cash on sending your film to every festival you find. First look for ones that specialize in youth. Next look for festivals that are for shorts. Get your work in as early as possible. Finally, seek out the ones that don't have a student entry fee.

When you apply to a festival, make sure to follow its guidelines. You don't want to be disqualified on a technical. At the same time, don't ever get too hung up on any one item in the application process.

Some festivals want copies of any press you have received as well as a still image from the movie (use your high-quality digital stills). Throw in a post card and an 8.5 x 11 poster. Be prepared to send in a list of your crew, a biography of yourself, and maybe even proof that you are a youth filmmaker.

Note to self: Festival coordinators hate envelopes that are padded with shredded paper. Use envelopes padded with air bubbles instead.

Most festivals want a summary of your film, and it is this along with your visuals that are the most important part of your application. Craft your summary like you crafted your movie — short and catchy.

If you have any questions, email the festival coordinator. As we have suggested throughout this whole book, play up the fact that you are a youth filmmaker. Impress upon him or her that you are a youth filmmaker who has his or her stuff together.

Check and see what the festival does with your film.

Read the fine print. We know of at least one festival that has you sign away the rights to your film for five years. This could be a bad or good thing depending on your perspective. On the one hand you personally cannot show it anymore. On the other, if they distribute it, it might get you noticed.

THE DIGITAL BAKE SALE: A WAY TO FUND YOUR NEXT FILM

You've got skills. And once the word gets around that you have these skills, you will become a prime target for everyone who wants a video of their football game or of their ballet recital. Here is how it will go down.

"Hey dude, I hear you have a camera. Can you film our game?" which turns into "Hey dude, can you edit our last ten games into a highlights reel for our banquet?" which turns into "Hey dude, can you make forty copies of this for the whole team?"

Your first thought is that you are honored. "Someone recognizes my skills!" Your next thought is "Where am I going to find time to do this and make my next film?" Your final thought should be "Show me the money."

But please don't say "Show me the money" to anyone's face.

Instead, make this proposal: You will film, edit, and make a DVD of their game, performance or whatever. Then sell the DVD to everyone on the team or in the club. You keep all the profits as payment for your services, or if you are feeling kind, let the club get some of the profits too. Overall this is a win-win situation. You get some cash and they get a professionally produced DVD. Do the math: 40 copies x $10 profit equals $400 in your pocket.

You are not limited to just games or performances. How about filming graduation, prom, or making a video yearbook? The video yearbook is a fast-growing trend that is really catching on all across the US. Students document the whole year and put it onto one DVD. It's a yearbook for the new millennium. You will even find that once you start to make one, people will be giving you footage that they shot just because they want it to be included.

While you may not get to keep the profits from a video yearbook for yourself, the money could go directly into a film program for your school. Do the math: 800 copies x $10 = $8,000. That's a lot of fancy film toys.

PRODUCTION AND REPRODUCTION

Remember, you are a filmmaker.

You have produced a film, and you might even know how to make a DVD on your computer, but don't make it your business to reproduce massive quantities of DVDs for your customers.

There are many reasons for avoiding DVD reproduction (or "duplication" if you are in the biz). First, reproducing large quantities of DVDs takes time. Plus, not all homemade DVDs play in all DVD players. Next, since you want the DVDs to look pro, they need a picture on the DVD (avoid stick-on labels). Finally, collecting cash from students with no cash can be difficult. You might get a lot more sales if moms and dads could just plop down their credit cards.

All of these problems can be fixed if you go with a service like Createspace.com. We have used them to distribute our own work and were very pleased. Buyers can order by phone or on the website with a credit card, and the only catch is that you share a little bit of the profit for each disk with them. The upside is that it is hassle free for you. Just send it away and they do all the work.

RESHOOT

Getting out there: Market your movie.

- ▶ Don't be shy or intimidated when it comes to submitting to festivals.
- ▶ Hold a local premiere of your film.
- ▶ Score the best LCD projector you can and crank the sound.
- ▶ Create posters, postcards, and tickets for your movie.
- ▶ Host a festival, create a website, and use a press release to create buzz/media attention.
- ▶ Be selective and read the fine print when submitting to festivals.
- ▶ The web and local cable access provide free distribution opportunities.
- ▶ Use your skills to make money for your next film.

CHAPTER **13**

YOUR DIGITAL
DISTRIBUTION
DEAL

Filmmaking techniques have been transformed by the advent of digital technology, but the changes in how we *make* film and video are minor when compared to the changes in the way we *watch* it.

Video has become portable, capable of going out into the world to find an audience in ways that were unimaginable just a few years ago. Your audience can now watch your work on a variety of screens, and in every imaginable location. Video is quite literally everywhere. This change creates huge opportunities and equally huge challenges. While it is now much simpler for the filmmaker to distribute his or her videos and gain access to a potentially huge viewing audience, the competition for "eyeballs" or "views" has grown exponentially more intense.

Dozens of hours of video are uploaded to the most popular sharing sites every minute. How can an aspiring filmmaker find a way to the viewers in this overwhelming tide of content? It certainly isn't simple or easy, but there are techniques and practices that can help your work bob to the surface of the video ocean.

YOUR DIGITAL DISTRIBUTION DEAL

Distribution used to be something you needed a "deal" to get. Something exclusive, required so your work would be displayed in theaters, on TV, or on DVD. Today, distribution is open to anyone, and means simply "where your video is available to be watched." Because there are so many virtual screening rooms or points of distribution that a filmmaker can take advantage of, a little thoughtful strategy can bring focus and, ultimately, a larger audience.

Where will send your videos in the digital universe?

YouTube. The word has become synonymous with online video, and while YouTube does have a huge audience, and the potential for creating a massive viral hit (about as likely as winning the lottery), it is certainly not the be-all and end-all when it comes to digital distribution. But is a good place to start.

GET TAGGED

Placing your video on any sharing site, YouTube included, will involve not only uploading a compressed version of your finished film, but also creating accompanying text information about your video. This text is referred to as "metadata" and usually consists of a title, a brief description, and keywords or "tags" that are associated with the subject matter of your movie.

Metadata is marketing — the most important free marketing campaign you may ever do. The title and description you give your video will serve to draw an audience. Those two elements combined with the tags will determine when your video will appear in answer to user searches (YouTube is owned by Google — optimizing search is key). So it is worth your time to craft your metadata carefully and with all the creativity you bring to filmmaking.

Clever or funny titles and descriptions are good when they work with the subject matter, but don't force funny titles on a serious show. Short titles without much descriptive information will work against you, so consider a "web only" title that is longer and contains more information. Use all the allotted characters or space for your description — this is free advertising! Max it out.

When adding tags, using unique words that suit your video will bring your video up in search results more often. Generic words like "funny," "hilarious," "great" or "amazing" will have little impact. In addition, tag all of your videos with something completely unique like your full name as one word, or a crazy word that you make up, or the name of your real or imaginary production company. Something that is "all you." These "branding tags" are important because on almost every video-sharing site, playing videos are displayed with an associated set of "related videos." Branding tags raise the likelihood that when one of your videos is playing, your other videos will be displayed alongside, ready for fans to dig deeper into your catalog. Use no more than a couple branding tags or the metadata on your videos will appear too similar, making them hard for search engines to distinguish.

Some less scrupulous filmmakers will try to game the system by including names of celebrities or sexual references in the metadata. While these techniques may bring a few additional views, it is a short-term strategy as you will alienate potentially loyal audience members, and generally damage your credibility.

Exercise: Practice creating eye and search-catching metadata for popular movies or TV shows with brief or one-word titles. How would you attract viewers to *Shrek*, *Gladiator*, *Saw*, or *Twilight*? Include a "Web Only" longer title, description and tags. Make sure that you include your personal branding tags.

CHANNEL SURFING

Everyone who publishes videos to YouTube (or to most web sharing sites) will automatically have their own "channel." This is essentially the page where all of your videos are collected and displayed. It is important that you personalize this page, so that the viewer is more likely to be immediately engaged by your content. The best customization isn't too busy and incorporates images you've developed (cast photos or poster images work well). Log in, then follow the "My Account" and "My Channel" tabs to the customization options.

If you have generated posters or fliers, these can be used to create a custom background. Production "stills" or snapshots of the set make for great backgrounds or wallpaper for your channel.

BE A COMMUNITY ORGANIZER

Once your channel is personalized, it's time to spread the word. Video sharing sites are "social media," environments where users expect to not only watch videos, but also to interact with the video creators and other viewers on the site. By creating relationships, you potentially increase viewership and raise your credibility as an online filmmaker. As a young person, however, you should be careful about the online "friendships" that you form. As with any online relationships, flag inappropriate behavior to the site itself, and inform adults immediately.

The most effective way to build an audience is to use the search features of YouTube and other web sharing sites to your benefit. Start by entering the key words you created for your video into the search bar. These results are important to you. These already popular and related videos are what your potential audience is currently watching. So get your name or video in front of them.

You can accomplish this by commenting with a link to your video and a suggestion to watch. You can also post your video as a "video response." Your video will have to be approved by the creator of the original video, but most will welcome your piece as a part of the conversation, as long as it is clearly related.

"Friending" the makers of similar videos is also a method for building community, but be careful to screen potential friends before adding them to your list (see above).

In the world of video sharing sites, good comments are pure gold. Comments on your video, especially positive comments and rankings, make your video much more interesting to the casual viewer. Action attracts viewers on YouTube, so the more comments the better. You should encourage commenting, but avoid replying to every comment that is left on your video. This kind of action brings more people in to see what is going on.

Should you delete negative comments? Not always. Comments are so valuable that having a negative comment or two is preferable to having none at all. Besides, negative comments can sometimes spark discussion or even controversy. This kind of conversation will bring increased viewership and exposure for your videos.

On the other hand, there are the notorious YouTube "Comment Trolls." The trolls are viewers that take pleasure in roaming around the site leaving rude, explicit, insulting comments. They are an unfortunate fact of life on video-sharing sites. It's part of the cost of putting your ideas out into the world. Delete them and move on.

Spam comments that do nothing more than direct viewers to another video, or offer some sketchy service should also be deleted as quickly as possible. Leaving these comments up will lead people to believe that the video creator does not pay attention to his or her videos on YouTube, and this is a turn-off to viewers who are looking for community as well as entertainment.

PADDING YOUR RESUME

One ingredient in YouTube success is also regular or frequent posting. This book is all about creating carefully polished and complete films, so for some filmmakers, creating a large number of videos goes against the grain. Don't let the temptation to post frequently bring down your production standards. Quality is the key to long-term success.

Instead of creating more movies, consider using a webcam to create a video blog or "vlog" about the progress of your production — a director's diary of the behind the scenes work. Each of these entries, with minimal editing, can be a fun accompaniment for your short. Also consider adding a "blooper reel" of goofs that took place on the set. Your viewers will love seeing this content after having seen the finished film.

In general, you can think of these as "extras" like those found on a DVD.

RUNNING NUMBERS

Posting videos to a big video-sharing site like YouTube can sometimes get a little discouraging. You release your work to the world, and wait for the views to pour in. You check back on your channel hourly, checking the statistics. Is there something wrong with YouTube? Your video has had less than a dozen views, and seems stuck. All that effort for a dozen views?

Take some consolation in this: Average views per month on a YouTube video as of this writing: 2. So a video with 12 views is 600% better than average! As hard as it may be, you need to be patient with your videos. Some take time to build audience and viewership. Some of the most famous "viral videos" languished on the site for months before finding a wide audience. Any video with more than 100 views in the first week should be considered a runaway hit.

Envision a movie theatre. The average movie theatre in this country has a capacity of between 200-300 viewers — or think of the auditorium at your school. How many people does it hold? When thinking of views, try measuring them in terms of sold-out theatre or auditoriums. 600 views may not feel like much when compared to the latest featured vid on the front page, but it's three sold-out shows at the local multiplex! Try to keep your expectations reasonable.

And be careful what you wish for. A front-page feature may get you hundreds of thousands of views, but that tsunami also brings with it a huge influx of comment trolls and spammers (see above), whereas the video that builds over time generally has a much more supportive and interested following.

THINKING OUTSIDE THE TUBE

While YouTube has the largest online viewership of any video sharing site by far, bigger is not always better. With so many videos pouring in, how can you get noticed by the editorial staff? How can influential viewers with lots of friends find you on such a huge site?

Some videos may be served better by being posted on niche sites that specialize in one type of video or another. Curated or collected video and short film sites may also be a good alternative, and ultimately end up yielding a bigger viewership.

As of this writing, there are several sites that specialize in humorous videos — Break.com, Crackle.com and FunnyorDie.com, just to name a few. If your film is comedy, or just has a few funny moments, consider posting here. Even generalized video sites with a smaller user base may be good. It's easier to get the attention of the editorial staff, and maybe snag a feature.

Given the number of video-sharing sites on the web, the aspiring filmmaker may soon find that they are spending all day just uploading and adding metadata. Adding videos to numerous locations can be extremely time consuming. Fortunately, there are a number of web video syndication sites and tools that can help streamline the syndication process. One of the most popular utilities for wider web distribution is offered by TubeMogul — and they even have a free option!

With TubeMogul and similar services, the producer needs to upload the video and metadata once, then the service compresses and sends the video to the various sharing sites. This can save hours worth of time with every video. There are potential problems in using a syndication service, however. It's very tempting to simply blast videos to every available point of distribution. Be selective. Only distribute to the number of sites that you think you can support (e.g. comment back) and only distribute to the sites you know are interested in your type of content. (Don't send your romantic comedy to a How-To site, even if you think there is instructional value in your film.)

RESHOOT

▶ New distribution options create opportunities and challenges.
▶ Metadata is marketing: be careful and creative with descriptions and titles.
▶ Your channel is your screening room: make yourself at home.
▶ Be patient with the numbers: how big is a theater, after all?
▶ Get beyond YouTube because other sites may serve you better.

CONCLUSION
FINAL CREDITS

Let's assume for a moment that you have followed all of our fine advice and finished a polished five-minute film. Let's presume that you've pulled off your shorts.

Congratulations are in order. Let's think about why what you have done is worthy of praise and admiration. Why is everyone so impressed?

Most people, non-filmmakers, will be amazed by your accomplishment, because while most folks have seen hundreds of films, they have only a vague idea about what goes into actually making one. To the average Josephine, you have managed a form of alchemy, a magic trick. They wish they knew the secrets, but they don't.

Despite not knowing the secrets of filmmaking, Joe Average Audience Member has incredibly high standards that he isn't even aware of. If you ask Joe, he will tell you that movies look like real life. By this point you know that isn't true. Home video looks like real life. Movies look like movies. Raised on Hollywood feature films, Joe is used to flawless framing, lighting, and sound. He's become an incredibly tough sell. In order to engage Joe's imagination, in order to get him to buy into the important creative message of your film, for him to be there for your art, you have to be a master of craft — the labor-intensive craft of filmmaking.

You've practiced that craft, from beginning to end. You've come up with a concept, written a script, produced, directed, edited, and marketed your film. You have been creative, collaborative, dedicated, overworked, amused, gratified, and applauded. You have been a diplomat, a banker, a carpenter, a huckster, an electrician, a geek, a manager, a weatherman, and an artist.

And now that you have pulled off your shorts, you are, in a sense, initiated into the select world of filmmakers. For better or worse, you've been Oz behind the curtain. You may never be a passive audience again. You will look at movies and television in an entirely new way. We think that's a good thing. You know all the elements that go into the process, the hundreds of hours, the huge variety of skills and tasks that go into making a film. Nobody can appreciate that in the way that another filmmaker can. So, come find us. Show us your movies. Talk to us. We can appreciate your craft.

But it isn't all about craft, about chasing away shadows with a shine board or getting the boom in just the right spot. There is also something completely unique in what you have done. Using an incredibly challenging medium, you have told your story. Even if in a small (or short) way, you have shared with the world your point of view. You have made a contribution to the world around you. And in that there is some genuine magic. Real Wizard of Oz stuff. Beauty and truth.

Good work if you can get it.

INDEX

ABOUT THE
AUTHORS

Troy Lanier   Clay Nichols

TROY LANIER produces documentary films. His documentary, *Streets Without Cars*, played on PBS stations across the U.S, and he has produced a series on the Pottery of Mexico. As a climber, Lanier also travels with and documents international climbing and caving expeditions. A graduate of the Georgia Institute of Technology, Lanier holds an MA from the University of Wisconsin in the History of Science. He has served as the director of the Devil's Canyon Wilderness Program and on the board of Proyecto Espeleologico Purificacion, an international organization dedicated to the exploration of Mexico's longest cave. He lives in Austin, Texas with his wife and children.

CLAY NICHOLS has written over a dozen plays for young and adult audiences that have been produced across the country. Titles include *Appleseed John*, *The Speaker Speaks*, and *The Nose in Exile*. His plays have received awards from the Center for American History at the University of Texas, the Austin Critics' Table, Playwrights' Center of San Francisco, and Stages Theatre of Houston. Nichols is a graduate of Dartmouth College and holds an MFA from the University of Texas where he was a James A. Michener Fellow at the Texas Center for Writers. During a twelve-year career in secondary schools, Nichols founded the Theatre Focus program at St. Stephen's School. He lives in Austin, Texas with his wife and three children.

Together, Nichols and Lanier are part of the founding team of DadLabs, a ground-breaking online video network. There they have produced over 500 video episodes that have been viewed millions of times worldwide.

SCREENWRITING FOR TEENS

THE 100 PRINCIPLES OF SCREENWRITING EVERY BUDDING WRITER MUST KNOW

CHRISTINA HAMLETT

This book gives teens — who go to movies more than any age group in the world — the tools to do more than just watch those movies: It gives them the tools to write their own films.

Targeted to the interests and vocabularies of junior high and high school students, each chapter of *Screenwriting for Teens* defines a concept, illustrates it with examples of current and/or classic films, and challenges its readers with creative writing, analytical, and discussion exercises. In addition to its value in a film-oriented curriculum, the material has application to coursework in English, Media, Theater, Journalism, and Psychology.

"For any writer looking for a different approach, this book offers dozens of possibilities — true and tested principles which millions of writers in the past have employed unconsciously, myself included."
> — John Collee, screenwriter, *Master and Commander: The Far Side of the World*

"This priceless jewel harbors the treasured secrets of how great screenplays are written and jump-starts your writing career with clear and truthful insight. It gives you a significant edge over other writers in this very competitive market. Buy two copies so that when one copy is worn from constant use and reference, you still have a spare."
> — Jennifer Farmer, director, producer, *Pumpkin Man, Naturally Native, Boomerang, Patience*

"Christina Hamlett's book is a marvel of clarity and helpfulness. Always simple, never simplistic: Complex topics are succinctly set forth at a level that today's sophisticated teens can easily understand, but never with a hint of condescension. I recommend it highly for anyone — teen OR adult — who wants not simply to play at 'making movies,' but to create quality, cinematic art."
> — Robert Parker, MM, DMA (High-School Teacher since 1985)

"Christina Hamlett's Screenwriting for Teens *is full of good advice for any novice writer, not just teens."*
> — Shannon Gardner, executive director, Young Filmmakers Academy

Former actress and director CHRISTINA HAMLETT is an award-winning author, instructor, and professional script coverage consultant whose credits to date include 24 books, 120 plays and musicals, 4 optioned feature films, and articles/interviews that appear in trade publications throughout the world. Prior screenwriting books include *Could It Be a Movie?* and *ScreenTEENwriters*.

$18.95 · 246 PAGES · ORDER NUMBER 62RLS · ISBN: 9781932907186

24 HOURS | **1.800.833.5738** | **WWW.MWP.COM**

MASTER SHOTS
100 ADVANCED CAMERA TECHNIQUES TO GET AN EXPENSIVE LOOK ON YOUR LOW BUDGET MOVIE

CHRISTOPHER KENWORTHY

Master Shots gives filmmakers the techniques they need to execute complex, original shots on any budget. By using powerful master shots and well-executed moves, directors can develop a strong style and stand out from the crowd. Most low-budget movies look low-budget, because the director is forced to compromise at the last minute. *Master Shots* gives you so many powerful techniques that you'll be able to respond, even under pressure, and create knock-out shots. Even when the clock is ticking and the light is fading, the techniques in this book can rescue your film, and make every shot look like it cost a fortune.

Each technique is illustrated with samples from great feature films and computer-generated diagrams for absolute clarity.

Use the secrets of the master directors to give your film the look and feel of a multi-million-dollar movie. The set-ups, moves and methods of the greats are there for the taking, whatever your budget.

"Master Shots *gives every filmmaker out there the blow-by-blow setup required to pull off even the most difficult of setups found from indies to the big Hollywood blockbusters. It's like getting all of the magician's tricks in one book."*
— Devin Watson, Producer, *The Cursed*

"Though one needs to choose any addition to a film book library carefully, what with the current plethora of volumes on cinema, Master Shots *is an essential addition to any worthwhile collection."*
— Scott Essman, Publisher, *Directed By* Magazine

"Christopher Kenworthy's book gives you a basic, no holds barred, no shot forgotten look at how films are made from the camera point of view. For anyone with a desire to understand how film is constructed — this book is for you."
— Matthew Terry, Screenwriter/Director, Columnist
www.hollywoodlitsales.com

Since 2000, CHRISTOPHER KENWORTHY has written, produced, and directed drama and comedy programs, along with many hours of commercial video, tv pilots, music videos, experimental projects, and short films. He's also produced and directed over 300 visual FX shots. In 2006 he directed the web-based Australian UFO Wave, which attracted many millions of viewers. Upcoming films for Kenworthy include *The Sickness* (2009) and *Glimpse* (2011).

$24.95 · 240 PAGES · ORDER NUMBER 91RLS · ISBN: 9781932907513

SETTING UP YOUR SHOTS, SECOND EDITION

GREAT CAMERA MOVES EVERY FILMMAKER SHOULD KNOW

JEREMY VINEYARD

This is the 2nd edition of one of the most successful filmmaking books in history, with sales of over 50,000 copies. Using examples from over 300 popular films, Vineyard provides detailed examples of more than 150 camera setups, angles, and moves which every filmmaker must know — presented in an easy-to-use "wide screen format." This book is the "Swiss Army Knife" that belongs in every filmmakers tool kit.

This new and revised 2nd edition of *Setting Up Your Shots* references over 200 new films and 25 additional filmmaking techniques.

This book gives the filmmaker a quick and easy "shot list" that he or she can use on the set to communicate with their crew.

The Shot List includes: Whip Pan, Reverse, Tilt, Helicopter Shot, Rack Focus, and much more.

"This is a film school in its own right and a valuable and worthy contribution to every filmmaker's shelf. Well done, Vineyard and Cruz!"
— Darrelyn Gunzburg, "For The Love Of It" Panel, *www.ForTheLoveOfIt.com*

"Perfect for any film enthusiast looking for the secrets behind creating film... It is a great addition to any collection for students and film pros alike....." Because of its simplicity of design and straight forward storyboards, this book is destined to be mandatory reading at films schools throughout the world."
— Ross Otterman, *Directed By* Magazine

"Setting Up Your Shots is a great book for defining the shots of today. The storyboard examples on every page make it an valuable reference book for directors and DP's alike! Great learning tool. Should be a boon for writers who want to choose the most effective shot and clearly show it in their boards for the maximum impact."
— Paul Clatworthy, Creator, StoryBoard Artist and StoryBoard Quick Software

JEREMY VINEYARD is currently developing an independent feature entitled "Concrete Road" with Keith David (*The Thing, Platoon*) and is working on his first novel, a modern epic.

$22.95 · 160 PAGES · ORDER NUMBER 84RLS · ISBN: 9781932907421

THE WRITER'S JOURNEY – 3RD EDITION
MYTHIC STRUCTURE FOR WRITERS

CHRISTOPHER VOGLER

BEST SELLER
OVER 180,000 COPIES SOLD!

See why this book has become an international best seller and a true classic. *The Writer's Journey* explores the powerful relationship between mythology and storytelling in a clear, concise style that's made it required reading for movie executives, screenwriters, playwrights, scholars, and fans of pop culture all over the world.

Both fiction and nonfiction writers will discover a set of useful myth-inspired storytelling paradigms (i.e., "The Hero's Journey") and step-by-step guidelines to plot and character development. Based on the work of Joseph Campbell, *The Writer's Journey* is a must for all writers interested in further developing their craft.

The updated and revised third edition provides new insights and observations from Vogler's ongoing work on mythology's influence on stories, movies, and man himself.

"This book is like having the smartest person in the story meeting come home with you and whisper what to do in your ear as you write a screenplay. Insight for insight, step for step, Chris Vogler takes us through the process of connecting theme to story and making a script come alive."
> – Lynda Obst, Producer, *Sleepless in Seattle, How to Lose a Guy in 10 Days*;
> Author, *Hello, He Lied*

"This is a book about the stories we write, and perhaps more importantly, the stories we live. It is the most influential work I have yet encountered on the art, nature, and the very purpose of storytelling."
> – Bruce Joel Rubin, Screenwriter, *Stuart Little 2, Deep Impact,*
> *Ghost, Jacob's Ladder*

CHRISTOPHER VOGLER is a veteran story consultant for major Hollywood film companies and a respected teacher of filmmakers and writers around the globe. He has influenced the stories of movies from *The Lion King* to *Fight Club* to *The Thin Red Line* and most recently wrote the first installment of *Ravenskull*, a Japanese-style manga or graphic novel. He is the executive producer of the feature film *P.S. Your Cat is Dead* and writer of the animated feature *Jester Till.*

$26.95 · 448 PAGES · ORDER NUMBER 76RLS · ISBN: 9781932907360

THE MYTH OF MWP

In a dark time, a light bringer came along, leading the curious and the frustrated to clarity and empowerment. It took the well-guarded secrets out of the hands of the few and made them available to all. It spread a spirit of openness and creative freedom, and built a storehouse of knowledge dedicated to the betterment of the arts.

The essence of the Michael Wiese Productions (MWP) is empowering people who have the burning desire to express themselves creatively. We help them realize their dreams by putting the tools in their hands. We demystify the sometimes secretive worlds of screenwriting, directing, acting, producing, film financing, and other media crafts.

By doing so, we hope to bring forth a realization of 'conscious media' which we define as being positively charged, emphasizing hope and affirming positive values like trust, cooperation, self-empowerment, freedom, and love. Grounded in the deep roots of myth, it aims to be healing both for those who make the art and those who encounter it. It hopes to be transformative for people, opening doors to new possibilities and pulling back veils to reveal hidden worlds.

MWP has built a storehouse of knowledge unequaled in the world, for no other publisher has so many titles on the media arts. Please visit www.mwp.com where you will find many free resources and a 25% discount on our books. Sign up and become part of the wider creative community!

Onward and upward,

Michael Wiese
Publisher/Filmmaker

AMITYVILLE PUBLIC LIBRARY